# Lightroom 1.0

## Student Manual

# Lightroom 1.0

| | |
|---|---|
| **President & Chief Executive Officer:** | Michael Springer |
| **Vice President, Product Development:** | Adam A. Wilcox |
| **Vice President, Operations:** | Josh Pincus |
| **Director of Publishing Systems Development:** | Dan Quackenbush |
| **Developmental Editor:** | Carl Pultz |
| **Copyeditor:** | Catherine Albano |
| **Keytester:** | Cliff Coryea |
| **Series Designer:** | Adam A. Wilcox |

## Trademarks

ILT Series is a trademark of Axzo Press.

Some of the product names and company names used in this book have been used for identification purposes only and may be trademarks or registered trademarks of their respective manufacturers and sellers.

## Disclaimer

We reserve the right to revise this publication and make changes from time to time in its content without notice.

Student Manual
ISBN-10: 1-4260-9983-5
ISBN-13: 978-1-4260-9983-0

Printed in the United States of America

1 2 3 4 5 GL 06 05 04 03

# Contents

# Introduction

After reading this introduction, you will know how to:

**A** Use Axzo Press ILT manuals in general.

**B** Use prerequisites, a target student description, course objectives, and a skills inventory to properly set your expectations for the course.

**C** Re-key this course after class.

# Topic A:  About the manual

### Axzo Press ILT Series philosophy

Our manuals facilitate your learning by providing structured interaction with the software itself. While we provide text to explain difficult concepts, the hands-on activities are the focus of our courses. By paying close attention as your instructor leads you through these activities, you will learn the skills and concepts effectively.

We believe strongly in the instructor-led class. During class, focus on your instructor. Our manuals are designed and written to facilitate your interaction with your instructor, and not to call attention to manuals themselves.

We believe in the basic approach of setting expectations, delivering instruction, and providing summary and review afterwards. For this reason, lessons begin with objectives and end with summaries. We also provide overall course objectives and a course summary to provide both an introduction to and closure on the entire course.

### Manual components

The manuals contain these major components:

- Table of contents
- Introduction
- Units
- Course summary
- Quick reference
- Glossary
- Index

Each element is described below.

#### Table of contents

The table of contents acts as a learning roadmap.

#### Introduction

The introduction contains information about our training philosophy and our manual components, features, and conventions. It contains target student, prerequisite, objective, and setup information for the specific course.

#### Units

Units are the largest structural component of the course content. A unit begins with a title page that lists objectives for each major subdivision, or topic, within the unit. Within each topic, conceptual and explanatory information alternates with hands-on activities. Units conclude with a summary comprising one paragraph for each topic, and an independent practice activity that gives you an opportunity to practice the skills you've learned.

The conceptual information takes the form of text paragraphs, exhibits, lists, and tables. The activities are structured in two columns, one telling you what to do, the other providing explanations, descriptions, and graphics.

### Course summary

This section provides a text summary of the entire course. It is useful for providing closure at the end of the course. The course summary also indicates the next course in this series, if there is one, and lists additional resources you might find useful as you continue to learn about the software.

### Quick reference

The quick reference is an at-a-glance job aid summarizing some of the more common features of the software.

### Glossary

The glossary provides definitions for all of the key terms used in this course.

### Index

The index at the end of this manual makes it easy for you to find information about a particular software component, feature, or concept.

## Manual conventions

We've tried to keep the number of elements and the types of formatting to a minimum in the manuals. This aids in clarity and makes the manuals more classically elegant looking. But there are some conventions and icons you should know about.

| Item | Description |
|------|-------------|
| *Italic text* | In conceptual text, indicates a new term or feature. |
| **Bold text** | In unit summaries, indicates a key term or concept. In an independent practice activity, indicates an explicit item that you select, choose, or type. |
| `Code font` | Indicates code or syntax. |
| `Longer strings of` ► `code will look` ► `like this.` | In the hands-on activities, any code that's too long to fit on a single line is divided into segments by one or more continuation characters (►). This code should be entered as a continuous string of text. |
| Select **bold item** | In the left column of hands-on activities, bold sans-serif text indicates an explicit item that you select, choose, or type. |
| Keycaps like (↵ ENTER) | Indicate a key on the keyboard you must press. |

## Hands-on activities

The hands-on activities are the most important parts of our manuals. They are divided into two primary columns. The "Here's how" column gives short instructions to you about what to do. The "Here's why" column provides explanations, graphics, and clarifications. Here's a sample:

*Do it!*

### A-1:   Creating a commission formula

| Here's how | Here's why |
|---|---|
| 1  Open Sales | This is an oversimplified sales compensation worksheet. It shows sales totals, commissions, and incentives for five sales reps. |
| 2  Observe the contents of cell F4 | F4 ▼   = =E4*C_Rate<br><br>The commission rate formulas use the name "C_Rate" instead of a value for the commission rate. |

For these activities, we have provided a collection of data files designed to help you learn each skill in a real-world business context. As you work through the activities, you will modify and update these files. Of course, you might make a mistake and therefore want to re-key the activity starting from scratch. To make it easy to start over, you will rename each data file at the end of the first activity in which the file is modified. Our convention for renaming files is to add the word "My" to the beginning of the file name. In the above activity, for example, a file called "Sales" is being used for the first time. At the end of this activity, you would save the file as "My sales," thus leaving the "Sales" file unchanged. If you make a mistake, you can start over using the original "Sales" file.

In some activities, however, it might not be practical to rename the data file. If you want to retry one of these activities, ask your instructor for a fresh copy of the original data file.

# Topic B:  Setting your expectations

Properly setting your expectations is essential to your success. This topic will help you do that by providing:

- Prerequisites for this course
- A description of the target student
- A list of the objectives for the course
- A skills assessment for the course

## Course prerequisites

Before taking this course, you should be familiar with personal computers and the use of a keyboard and a mouse. Furthermore, this course assumes that you've completed the following course or have equivalent experience:

- *Windows XP: Basic*

## Target student

Adobe Photoshop Lightroom is designed specifically for digital photographers who are looking for a streamlined approach to managing, editing, and presenting their photos. You might have some experience with Photoshop, or other photo-editing or photo-management applications, but no specific level of exposure is necessary in order to complete the course.

## Course objectives

These overall course objectives will give you an idea about what to expect from the course. It is also possible that they will help you see that this course is not the right one for you. If you think you either lack the prerequisite knowledge or already know most of the subject matter to be covered, you should let your instructor know that you think you are misplaced in the class.

After completing this course, you will know how to:

- Explore the basics of the Lightroom interface; import photos and set various import options; change views in the library and make basic adjustments; adjust the Lightroom interface; and use keyboard shortcuts to improve efficiency.

- Flag, rate, stack, sort, and cull photos by using Survey view; create and manipulate keywords; create collections; filter photos in Grid view; and synchronize develop settings and metadata adjustments within groups of photos.

- Apply presets to photos, adjust white balance, make basic tonal adjustments, use history steps to revert to previous versions of photos, create snapshots, compare before and after versions of photos, adjust tone curves, make precise shadow and highlight adjustments, adjust color, convert photos to grayscale, create split-tone effects, crop and straighten photos, make precise detail adjustments, copy and paste adjustments between photos, and create custom presets.

- Preview a slideshow, adjust basic slide and backdrop options, save custom slideshow settings as a template, add text overlays to slides, adjust the size and placement of photos, adjust playback options for a slideshow, and export a slideshow as a PDF.

- Adjust the way photos are arranged on pages, including single photo layouts and multiple photo layouts; and adjust output settings, including basic printing options and color management options.

- Create a Flash-based web gallery, including adding text, adjusting layout and colors, and adding photo information; preview a web gallery and upload it to a host server.

## Skills inventory

Use the following form to gauge your skill level entering the class. For each skill listed, rate your familiarity from 1 to 5, with 5 being the most familiar. *This is not a test.* Rather, it is intended to provide you with an idea of where you're starting from at the beginning of class. If you're wholly unfamiliar with all the skills, you might not be ready for the class. If you think you already understand all of the skills, you might need to move on to the next course in the series. In either case, you should let your instructor know as soon as possible.

| Skill | 1 | 2 | 3 | 4 | 5 |
|---|---|---|---|---|---|
| Exploring file handling options during import | | | | | |
| Exploring segmenting options | | | | | |
| Processing imported files | | | | | |
| Importing photos via a watched folder | | | | | |
| Viewing photos in the Library | | | | | |
| Adjusting interface elements | | | | | |
| Creating an identity plate | | | | | |
| Navigating by using shortcuts | | | | | |
| Flagging photos | | | | | |
| Rating and sorting photos | | | | | |
| Stacking photos | | | | | |
| Culling by using Survey view | | | | | |
| Assigning and manipulating keywords | | | | | |
| Creating a collection | | | | | |
| Adding photos to a Quick Collection | | | | | |
| Finding photos | | | | | |
| Synchronizing photos | | | | | |
| Manipulating metadata | | | | | |
| Exporting photos | | | | | |
| Applying presets | | | | | |
| Adjusting white balance | | | | | |
| Adjusting tonal range | | | | | |

| Skill | 1 | 2 | 3 | 4 | 5 |
|---|---|---|---|---|---|
| Working with the History and Snapshots panels | | | | | |
| Comparing before and after versions of photos | | | | | |
| Adjusting tones by using a tone curve | | | | | |
| Adjusting shadows and highlights | | | | | |
| Adjusting specific colors | | | | | |
| Converting a photo to grayscale and split toning a photo | | | | | |
| Cropping and straightening photos | | | | | |
| Controlling photo detail | | | | | |
| Copying and pasting adjustments | | | | | |
| Creating a Develop preset | | | | | |
| Viewing basic slideshows | | | | | |
| Adjusting slide options and backdrop settings | | | | | |
| Creating slideshow templates | | | | | |
| Adding an identity plate | | | | | |
| Adding slideshow text overlays | | | | | |
| Choosing playback settings for slideshows | | | | | |
| Viewing and exporting slideshows | | | | | |
| Adjusting basic print settings | | | | | |
| Setting up a multi-photo layout | | | | | |
| Setting up a specific size print | | | | | |
| Rotating prints | | | | | |
| Setting up borderless prints | | | | | |
| Choosing basic print settings | | | | | |
| Printing with Lightroom-controlled color management | | | | | |
| Printing with printer-controlled color management | | | | | |
| Creating a basic web gallery | | | | | |

| Skill | 1 | 2 | 3 | 4 | 5 |
|---|---|---|---|---|---|
| Customizing a web gallery | | | | | |
| Adding information to photos | | | | | |
| Previewing and uploading a web gallery | | | | | |

# Topic C:  Re-keying the course

If you have the proper hardware and software, you can re-key this course after class. This section explains what you'll need in order to do so, and how to do it.

## Hardware requirements

Your personal computer should have:

- A keyboard and a mouse
- Intel Pentium 4 processor or better (Conversion and rendering can be very processor intensive, so a faster processor is recommended)
- 768 MB of RAM (1 GB recommended)
- 1GB of available hard-disk space in addition to the operating system
- A CD-ROM drive
- A monitor capable of displaying 1,024×768 pixels at Highest (32 bit) color quality

## Software requirements

You will also need the following software:

- Windows XP with Service Pack 2
- Adobe Photoshop Lightroom v. 1.4.1 or later
- Epson Stylus Photo 2400R inkjet printer driver software, downloaded from the Internet
- Adobe Flash player, downloaded from the Internet
- Adobe Reader, downloaded from the Internet

## Network requirements

The following network components and connectivity are also required for rekeying this course:

- Internet access, for the following purposes:
  - Downloading the latest critical updates and service packs from www.windowsupdate.com
  - Downloading supplementary software
  - Downloading the student data files (if necessary)

## Setup instructions to re-key the course

Before you re-key the course, you will need to perform the following steps.

1 Download the latest critical updates and service packs from www.windowsupdate.com.

2 From the Control Panel, open the Display Properties dialog box and apply the following settings:

- Theme — Windows XP
- Screen resolution — 1024 by 768 pixels
- Color quality — High (24 bit) or higher

If you choose not to apply these display settings, your screens might not match the screen shots in this manual.

3 Display file extensions and hidden files.

   a Start Windows Explorer.

   b Choose Tools, Folder Options, and select the View tab.

   c Clear the check box for Hide extensions for known file types.

   d Select Show hidden files and folders, and click OK.

   e Close Windows Explorer.

4 Delete all files from the following folders (not the folders themselves) to reset any defaults that have been changed in previous uses of Lightroom, if necessary. (For a standard hard drive setup, the primary hard drive will be C:\). (You might wish to save these folders elsewhere rather than deleting them.)

   a C:\Documents and Settings\<Current User>\Application Data\Adobe\Lightroom\Develop Presets

   b C:\Documents and Settings\<Current User>\Application Data\Adobe\Lightroom\Metadata Presets

   c C:\Documents and Settings\<Current User>\Application Data\Adobe\Lightroom\Slideshow Presets

   d C:\Documents and Settings\<Current User>\Application Data\Adobe\Lightroom\Print Presets

   e C:\Documents and Settings\<Current User>\Application Data\Adobe\Lightroom\Preferences

5 Delete the Lightroom folder, if present, from the C:\Documents and Settings\<Current User>\My Documents\My Pictures folder to force Lightroom to create a new library when opened.

6 Download and install the printer driver for the Epson Stylus Photo R2400 inkjet printer to create a "virtual printer" (one that you can select in the Print dialog box without having the physical printer connected), as follows:

   a Navigate to the downloads page for the printer at www.epson.com.

   b Download the most recent version of the printer driver for your operating system. At the time of this writing, the file for Windows XP was epson12110.exe.

   c Run the installer.

   d In the WinZip Self-Extractor dialog box, click Unzip.

   e Follow prompts in the installer dialog boxes.

   f In the EPSON Printer Utilities Setup dialog box, click Manual (unless you have this specific printer, in which case you can simply connect it).

   g Under Available Ports, select USB001 (Virtual printer port for USB).

   h Click OK when prompted.

7 Download and install the glossy paper ICC profiles for the Epson Stylus Photo R2400 inkjet printer. The profiles are available at the same location on the Epson Web site as the printer driver.

   a Navigate to the downloads page for the printer at www.epson.com.

   b Download the ICC profiles for glossy paper. At the time of this writing, the file for Windows XP was epson11713.exe.

   c Run the installer.

   d In the WinZip Self-Extractor dialog box, click Unzip.

   e Follow prompts in the installer dialog boxes.

8 Download and install the current Flash Player from www.adobe.com.

9 Download and install the current Adobe Reader from www.adobe.com. Open Adobe Reader and accept the license agreement, then close the program.

10 Configure Internet Explorer to display active content.

   a Open Internet Explorer and choose Tools, Internet Options.

   b On the Advanced tab, under Security, check Allow active content to run in files on My Computer.

   c Click OK.

   d Close Internet Explorer.

11 Create a folder named Student Data at the root of the hard drive. For a standard hard drive setup, this will be C:\Student Data.

12 Copy the data files from the disk supplied with this book to the Student Data folder

This page intentionally left blank.

# Unit 1

## Getting started

**Unit time: 60 minutes**

Complete this unit, and you'll know how to:

**A** Discuss Lightroom workflows and explore the basics of the Lightroom interface.

**B** Import photos and set import options.

**C** Change views in the library and make basic adjustments.

**D** Adjust the Lightroom interface and use keyboard shortcuts to improve efficiency.

# Topic A: Lightroom overview

*Explanation*

Adobe Lightroom is designed specifically for digital photographers to help them streamline the way they manage, adjust, and present large volumes of digital photographs. Its strength lies in its ability to improve your workflow, from importing photos to outputting them in a variety of formats. You can use Lightroom to quickly manipulate entire libraries, or drill down to work with specific photos, such as those from your latest shoot.

## The Lightroom workflow

If you've worked with digital photos, you've likely already developed your own personal workflow, which could include your own way of organizing and tracking photos. The exact workflow you use in Lightroom is somewhat flexible, and it's likely you'll be able to incorporate many of your own techniques. A typical workflow could include:

- Adding a "shoot" or series of photos to your library.
- Sorting through photos, perhaps ranking them based on content and quality.
- Making photo adjustments as necessary. This could include white balance adjustments, color correction, tonal range improvements, contrast adjustments, or cropping and straightening.
- Outputting photos, if necessary. Lightroom includes modules for generating slideshows, printing, exporting to other formats, and creating web galleries.

### JPEG vs. Camera RAW

Lightroom can handle a variety of file types, but most digital cameras output high-quality photos typically saved in the JPEG format. This is the format routinely used to display photographic images on the Web. However, some digital cameras, especially high-end cameras, can output photographs as camera RAW files. As its name suggests, the camera RAW format outputs the image data directly from the camera's sensor without applying any processing or compression.

In contrast, when you shoot photos as JPEGs, your camera applies post-processing to the photo based on the camera's settings, and compresses it to reduce file size. The JPEG format is suitable for most amateur photographers, but to get the highest possible quality, you should use the camera RAW format.

The following table delineates some of the differences between the two.

| Issue | JPEG | Camera RAW |
|---|---|---|
| Image processing | Cameras process JPEG photos within the camera. Some of the processing is destructive. For example, some fine details in the photo might be obscured even at the highest quality setting. | Camera RAW photos have little or no compression, so they're very clean and free of artifacts. Any post-processing specified by the camera isn't performed but is stored as metadata—that is, data about the photo—with the photo itself. |
| White balance | Cameras automatically apply white balance to JPEGs. If you set a camera to Daylight white balance, but shoot pictures inside, they'll likely look somewhat orange, because tungsten lights are more red-orange than daylight. You can adjust it after the fact with a JPEG photo, but it can be hard to completely fix, as the Red color channel may have clipped information (maxed some of the pixels at 255). | Camera RAW files don't have white balance applied to them. Only when you open the files with a RAW converter (such as Lightroom) is the white balance applied. So if you make a mistake setting the white balance when you take the picture, you can easily change it within Lightroom. |
| Photo adjustments | Photo adjustments can be more difficult with JPEGs. For example, you might expect initially to create a small print, and set your camera to a high level of sharpening. But if you decide to print it large, you might see "halos" at edges because of that choice. | Because very little processing is applied to Camera RAW files, photo adjustments are much easier and more accurate. For example, with Camera RAW files, you control how much sharpening you want during conversion. |

It's also important to note that any adjustments you make in Lightroom are non-destructive to your photos. For example, if you convert a photo to grayscale or make a lot of adjustments to it, the changes are visible only in Lightroom. Should you open the photo in another application, it will be exactly as it was when you downloaded it from your camera.

## The Lightroom interface

The Lightroom interface consists of five basic elements, as shown in Exhibit 1-1. On the right and left sides are panel groups, which display a variety of panels depending on the module you're working with. The center pane shows the photos you've imported within a grid, and it also shows larger versions of selected photos as you work. You can change the grid layout, and switch views to focus on an individual photo, or a smaller group of photos. At the bottom of the window is the Filmstrip, which horizontally shows the photos you've imported. The Filmstrip is available regardless of the view you select in the center pane. The top-right corner shows five modules, which you can select to perform different tasks with your photos. The active module appears white. To switch to another module, click its name.

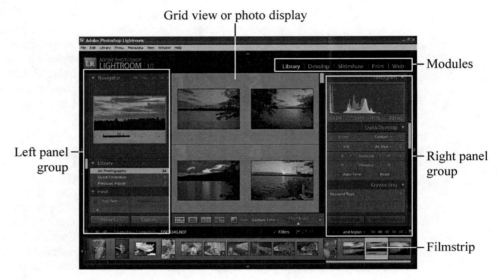

*Exhibit 1-1: The Lightroom interface*

**Modules**

When you import photos in Lightroom, they are visible by default in the Library module. The following table briefly describes each Lightroom module.

| Module | Description |
|---|---|
| Library | (Default) Used to organize, preview, and apply basic adjustments to photos. You can also add or edit keywords and metadata. |
| Develop | Used to make more advanced adjustments to photos, including white balance, tonal curves, color adjustments, split toning, camera calibration, and cropping and straightening photos. |
| Slideshow | Used to create and modify slideshows. You can select photos to include, set slideshow properties such as background color, slideshow layout and drop shadows, as well as set playback controls. |
| Print | Used to prepare photo collections for printing. You can set page attributes, including the number of photos per sheet and the overall layout, as well as basic color management settings. |
| Web | Used to generate online web galleries. You can create HTML- or Flash-based galleries, control photo size and gallery layout, and determine whether to include photo titles and captions. |

*Do it!*

## A-1:   Discussing Lightroom

### Questions and answers

1   Which file format provides you with the cleanest photos to work with?

2   What characteristics of Camera RAW files make them easier to adjust?

3   What are the five modules you can use in Lightroom?

4   How can you switch modules?

5   Which interface element is visible regardless of the module you're working with?

# Topic B: Importing photos

*Explanation*

To begin using Lightroom, you need to import photos to work with. There are various ways to do this. For example, you can import a selection of photos, or you can opt to import an entire folder. You can also set options for photos as you import them, such as how they are named, whether they have metadata attached, or how they look.

### The Five Rules window

The first time you launch Lightroom, you're presented with the Five Rules window, shown in Exhibit 1-2. The window provides some starter information about Modules, Panels, the Filmstrip, and a few useful keyboard shortcuts. Click Next to view each of the five rules, or Finish to close the window and view the Lightroom interface. The Five Rules window will not appear again the next time you launch the application. If you want to view the five rules again, you'll need to choose Help, The Five Rules.

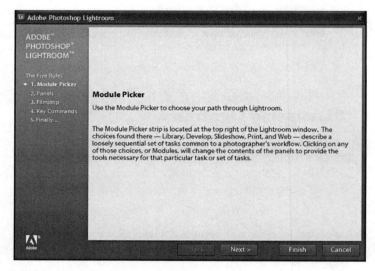

*Exhibit 1-2: The Five Rules window*

### Import photos

To import photos:

1 In the bottom-left corner of the left panel group, click Import. You can also choose File, Import, or press Ctrl+Shift+I. The Open dialog box appears.

2 Navigate to the location of the folder containing the photos you want to import and do one of the following:

 • If you want to import specific photos, select the photos and click Open.

 • If you want to import an entire folder of photos, select the folder and click Choose Selected.

 In either case the Import Photos dialog box appears, as shown in Exhibit 1-3.

3 Set the options you want for the imported photos and click Import.

**The Import Photos dialog box**

You can change the location of the photo files as you import them, or specify that Lightroom reference the files from their current location. Each approach has its advantages. If you currently maintain a specific folder structure, you can keep the same structure. This is especially useful if you already store photos in different locations and on different drives. Alternately, if you want to maintain a library in one specific location, you can instruct Lightroom to move the photos. If you select this option, Lightroom stores the photos in a new Lightroom folder within the My Pictures folder on your computer. You can also rename photos as you move them.

*Exhibit 1-3: File handling options in the Import Photos dialog box*

**Preview photos**

The Import Photos dialog box also provides a preview for the photos you import, as shown in Exhibit 1-3. To view previews, check Show Preview in the lower-left corner. If you are importing a folder or group of photos, you can change the size of the previews by dragging the preview slider.

*Do it!*

## B-1: Exploring basic photo importing options

| Here's how | Here's why |
|---|---|
| 1 Start Lightroom | (Click Start and choose All Programs, Adobe Photoshop Lightroom, Adobe Photoshop Lightroom.) If this is the first time you've launched Lightroom, the Five Rules window appears, asking if you want Lightroom to automatically check for updates. |
| 2 Verify that Automatic is selected and click **Next** | To advance to the first of the five rules. |
| 3 Read the first rule and click **Next** | To advance through the five rules. As you read the rules, certain parts of the Lightroom interface are highlighted. |
| Continue advancing through the five rules | |
| After you read the last rule, click **Finish** | |
| 4 In the upper-right corner of the interface, verify that the Library module is active | The selected module name appears in white characters. (If it is not active, click Library to make it active.) You'll import some photos. |
| 5 In the bottom-left corner of the left panels group, click **Import** | |
| | To open the Open dialog box. |
| Navigate to the Media folder | In the Student Data folder. |
| 6 Select **2005-08-02 Lake** | You'll import the entire folder. |
| 7 Click **Choose Selected** | The Import Photos dialog box appears. You'll explore each file-handling option to see the possible benefits of each. |
| 8 Observe the two subfolders in the list | The subfolders each contain photos. The Lake folder has eight photos and the Waterfall folder has seven. |
| 9 In the bottom-left corner, click **Show Preview** | The dialog box width expands and previews of the photos are visible on the right side. |

10  Scroll down to view all the thumbnail previews

By default, Lightroom shows previews for the first folder in the list.

11  Under File Handling, select the Waterfall folder

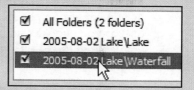

The previews on the right change to show the photos in this folder.

12  Under the previews, drag the preview slider slightly to the left

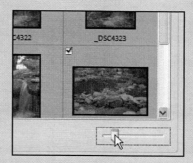

To decrease the size of the previews.

## Organization and file-naming options

*Explanation*

As you import photos, you can specify how they are organized. For example, you can import photos so that they retain the same folder hierarchy you have on your hard drive, or you can group photos based on the date they were taken. Organization options appear only if you choose to move the photos you're importing to a new location. They are available in the File Handling section of the Import Photos dialog box, as shown in Exhibit 1-4.

You can also rename files if you're moving them to a new location. To do this, select a file-naming template from the list in the File Naming section shown in Exhibit 1-4. You can select from several file-naming templates, or you can create your own naming conventions.

Organization options —

File naming — options

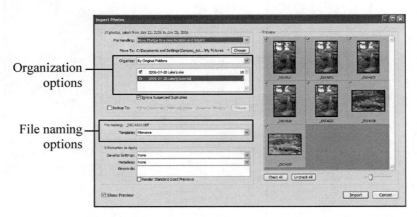

*Exhibit 1-4: Organization and file-naming options in the Import Photos dialog box*

### The Folders and Library panels

After you import photos, they appear in Grid view in the center pane, and new folders become visible in the Folders panel, shown in Exhibit 1-5. If a folder contains subfolders, they are included as well. To view subfolders, click the small triangle to the left of the folder name.

*Exhibit 1-5: The Folders panel*

As you import more and more photos, you can navigate them by clicking the folder titles in the Folders panel. When you select a folder, only the photos within that folder are visible in the center pane. If you want to view all the photos in your library, you need to click All Photographs in the Library panel, shown in Exhibit 1-6. You can also view the last photos you imported by clicking Previous Import.

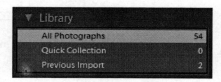

*Exhibit 1-6: The Library panel*

*Do it!*

## B-2: Exploring organization and file-naming options

| Here's how | Here's why |
|---|---|
| 1 From the File Handling list, select **Move photos to a new location and Import** | File Handling: Import Photos at their Current Location<br><br>Import Photos at their Current Location<br>Copy Photos to a new location and Import<br>Move Photos to a new location and Import<br>Copy Photos as Digital Negative (DNG) and Import<br><br>The dialog box expands to show additional options. |
| 2 From the Organize list, select **By Date: 2005/12-17** | To specify a date format to display the photos. Lightroom examines the photos in the subfolders and organizes them by date. The photos were taken on two different dates. Ten were taken on 8/01 and five were taken on 8/02. |
| 3 Observe the previews on the right | The photos are mixed now. All of the lake photos are visible, as well as two pond photos that were in the Waterfall folder. |
| 4 From the Organize list, select **By Original Folders** | To return to the default folder scheme. You like this organization scheme, so you'll keep it.<br><br>You'll experiment with file-renaming options that are allowed if you move photos to a new location. |
| 5 Under File Naming, from the Template list, select **Date – Filename** | File Naming: 20050801-DSC_4334.NEF<br><br>Template: Date - Filename<br><br>The file name example above the list now shows the date the photo was taken followed by the current file name.<br><br>You decide that it would be more convenient to leave the photos in their current locations than to move them to a new location. |
| 6 From the File Handling list, select **Import Photos at their Current Location** | The organization and file-handling options are no longer visible. |
| 7 Click **Import** | The photos appear in the library in Grid view and also in the Filmstrip. |
| 8 In the left panel group, scroll down | ▼ Folders                +<br>▷ 2005-08-02 Lake       15<br><br>To view the Folders panel. The folder you originally selected is visible. |

| | |
|---|---|
| 9  In the center pane, scroll down to view all the photos | All the lake and waterfall photos are visible. |
| 10  In the Folders panel, click as shown |  |
| | To expand the 2005-08-02 Lake folder. The Lake and Waterfall subfolders appear indented beneath the one you expanded. |
| Click **Lake** | To display only the pictures of the lake. |
| Click **Waterfall** | To display only the waterfall photos. |
| 11  Click **2005-08-02 Lake** | To display all 15 photos again. |
| 12  Import files from the Prior shoots folder, referencing files in their existing locations | Click Import, select the Prior shoots folder, click Choose Selected, verify that Import Photos at their Current Location is selected, and click Import. |
| 13  Observe the Folders panel |  |
| | A new folder titled Prior shoots is visible. |
| Expand Prior shoots | (In the Folders panel, click the small triangle to the left of Prior shoots.) To view the subfolders. |
| 14  In the left panel group, scroll up to view the Library panel | |
| 15  In the panel, click **All Photographs** |  |
| | To display all the photos you've imported. |
| In the center pane, scroll down | To view all 51 photos. |

## Processing options

*Explanation*

Sometimes you might want to attach information to photos as you import them, or specify a develop setting so that photos appear a certain way, such as grayscale or with a sepia tone. You can do this by selecting options in the Information to Apply section of the Import Photos dialog box, shown in Exhibit 1-7.

Attaching information or *metadata* to photos provides an effective way for photographers to manage their collections. Lightroom lets you attach metadata by using a catalog system created by the *IPTC (International Press Telecommunications Council)*. This system was established as a way to help photographers organize and market their work. There is a vast range of information you can include, such as your name, copyright statements, license information, captions, and keywords. Embedding this information allows you to easily perform searches for specific photos. It can also make image usage and licensing simpler to track.

Processing options →

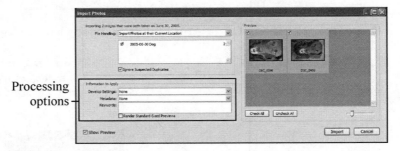

*Exhibit 1-7: Processing options in the Import Photos dialog box*

You can add ITPC metadata as you import photos, or to photos already included in your library. However, some types of information, such as your name or a copyright statement are easier to add as you import them, and you can specify that Lightroom automatically add them.

To add ITPC metadata to all photos:

1 In the Import Photos dialog box, select New from the Metadata list in the Information to Apply section. When you do, the New Metadata Preset dialog box appears, as shown in Exhibit 1-8.

2 In the Preset Name box, enter a descriptive name for the new metadata information.

3 Fill in the metadata information you want. Each time you enter information in a field, a checkmark appears to the right, indicating it will be attached to the photos.

4 Click Create to return to the Import Photos dialog box.

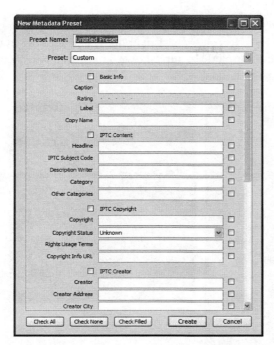

*Exhibit 1-8: The New Metadata Preset dialog box*

**The Keywords and Metadata panels**

After you import photos with metadata information applied, you can verify the information is correct by selecting one of the photos and looking at the Keywording and Metadata panels in the right panel group, shown in Exhibit 1-9. You can also use the panels to add or change metadata.

*Exhibit 1-9: The Metadata and Keywording panels*

*Do it!*

### B-3: Processing imported files

| Here's how | Here's why |
|---|---|
| 1 Click **Import** | To begin importing more photos. This time, you'll apply keywords and metadata to the files as you import them. |
| Select **2005-07-06 Black Labrador** | |
| 2 Click **Choose Selected** | To select the folder and open the Import Photos dialog box. |
| 3 Verify that "Import Photos at their current Location" is selected | |

4 Under Information to Apply, in the Keywords box, enter **Dogs, Animals**, as shown

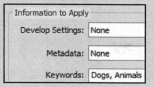

To add two keywords to the photos. You'll also add a copyright statement.

5 From the Metadata list, select **New…**

To open the New Metadata Preset dialog box.

6 In the Preset Name box, enter **My copyright**

To name the preset you'll create.

7 Under IPTC Copyright, in the Copyright box, enter **Copyright <Current year> <Student Name>**

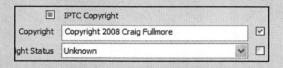

Enter your name and the current year for the text specified within the brackets.

8 Scroll down to view IPTC Creator codes

Enter the information shown, ensuring that each item is checked when complete

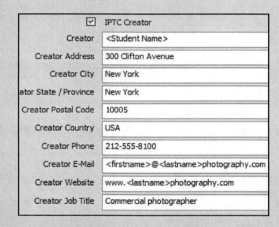

Click **Create**

To complete the Metadata preset.

9 Click **Import**

To import the photos.

10 Observe the photos in the center pane

Both dog photos show small keyword badges in the lower-right corners.

| | | |
|---|---|---|
| 11 | Click the first photo | To select it. |
| 12 | In the right panel group, scroll down to view the Keywording and Metadata panels | Some of the information you entered for the photos is visible. You'll import more photos and apply the same copyright metadata to them. |
| 13 | Display the photos in the 2005-08-14 Restaurateur folder in the Import Photos dialog box | Click Import, navigate to the 2005-08-14 Restaurateur folder, and click Choose Selected. |
| 14 | In the Information to Apply section, verify that My copyright is selected in the Metadata list | The settings you chose last still apply, so you'll need to remove the keywords. |
| 15 | Remove the Dogs and Animals keywords in the Keywords box | You'll also convert these photos to grayscale as you import them. |
| 16 | From the Develop Settings list, select **General - Grayscale** | To convert both files in this shoot to grayscale. |
| | Click **Import** | To import the files. At first, the photos appear in color. However, after a few seconds, the photos switch to grayscale. |
| 17 | In the left panel group, scroll up to view the Library panel | If necessary. |
| | In the panel, click **All Photographs** | To display all photos. |

## Automatically importing from a watched folder

*Explanation*

You can also set Lightroom to automatically import photos each time they are added to a specific folder on your computer. When you use this option, Lightroom automatically copies the photos to a managed folder on your computer. To automatically import photos from a watched folder:

1  Choose File, Auto Import, Enable Auto Import.

2  Choose File, Auto Import, Auto Import Settings to open the Auto Import Settings dialog box, shown in Exhibit 1-10.

3  To the right of Watched Folder, click Choose and navigate to the folder you want to set as the watched folder. Select the folder and click OK.

4  In the Destination section, specify a managed destination folder for the photos. You can also specify a descriptive name for it. By default, Lightroom creates a folder in the My Pictures folder on your computer.

5  In the Filenaming and Information sections, specify a file-naming convention and processing settings for the photos, if necessary. These options are optional.

6  Click OK to apply the settings.

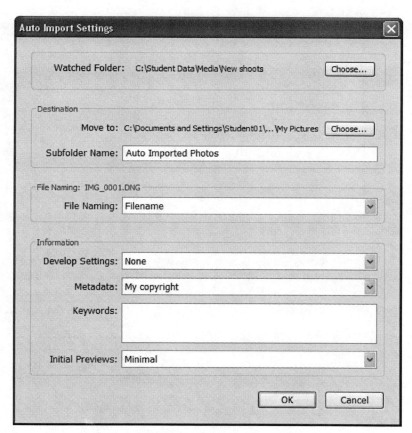

*Exhibit 1-10: The Auto Import Settings dialog box*

### Renaming folders

Each time you add photos from a watched folder, they appear in the Folders panel titled Auto Imported Photos. You can rename the folder by double-clicking it and entering a more descriptive title.

## B-4: Importing photos from a watched folder

| Here's how | Here's why |
|---|---|
| 1 Choose **File**, **Auto Import**, **Auto Import Settings** | To open the Auto Import Settings dialog box. |
| 2 To the right of Watched Folder, click **Choose** | To select the watched folder. |
| 3 Navigate to the Media folder | Within the current Student Data folder, if necessary. |
| Select **New shoots** | |
| Click **OK** | Watched Folder:  C:\Student Data\Media\New shoots |
| | To select the folder and return to the dialog box. |
| 4 In the File Naming section, verify that Filename is selected | To retain the original photo file names. |
| 5 In the Information section, from the Metadata list, select **My copyright** | To apply your copyright information to each automatically imported photo. |
| Verify that the settings are as shown in Exhibit 1-10 | |
| Click **OK** | To accept the settings. |
| 6 Minimize Adobe Lightroom | You'll drag files to the watched folder in Windows Explorer. |
| 7 In Windows Explorer, navigate to the 2005-08-14 Children folder | In the Media folder within the Student Data folder. |
| 8 Click **Folders** | Search  Folders  \|▦▾\| |
| | (If necessary.) To display the folder tree on the left side of the Windows Explorer window. |
| Press CTRL + A | To select all six of the photos in the folder. |
| Drag the selected files to the New shoots folder | |
| 9 Restore Adobe Lightroom | Click its taskbar button. |
| 10 In the left panel, scroll down to the Folders panel | To display the imported folders. |

| | | |
|---|---|---|
| 11 | Choose **File, Auto Import, Enable Auto Import** | The Auto Imported Photos folder appears in the list. |
| | Observe the value to the right of All Photographs in the Library panel | If you return quickly enough, the number will increase as the photos are imported. |
| 12 | In the Folders panel, click **Auto Imported Photos** | To display the six photos that were imported automatically when you moved them to the watched folder. |

# Topic C: Viewing photos

*Explanation*

After you've imported photos, you can change the way they are presented in the center pane. Changing views makes it easier to analyze and compare photos, and to make adjustments, if necessary.

## Grid options

By default, photos appear in the Library module in Grid view (in the center pane). Each photo shows an index number in the upper-left corner, as shown in Exhibit 1-11. Index numbers are grid-specific, not photo specific. For example, the top-left photo in the grid will always be number 1, regardless of the view or folder you're looking at.

*Exhibit 1-11: A photo in default Grid view in the Library module*

You can change the information visible in Grid view by pressing "j" on the keyboard. There are three Grid views: the default view showing only the index numbers, the photos with extended information, and the photos with no information.

## Library view modes

You can switch views in the Library module to focus on one photo, or a series of specific photos. In the toolbar at the bottom of the center pane are four view mode buttons: Grid, Loupe, Compare, and Survey. To the right of the buttons are options that correspond to the view you've selected, as shown in Exhibit 1-12. In Grid view, you can change the way the photos are sorted, or change the size of the photo thumbnails. In Loupe view you can magnify, rotate, and rate photos. In Compare view, you can perform side-by-side comparisons of two selected photos. In Survey view, you can select and compare three or more photos.

View mode buttons

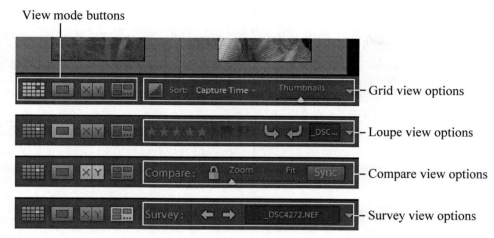

— Grid view options

— Loupe view options

— Compare view options

— Survey view options

*Exhibit 1-12: View mode buttons and options in the toolbar in Library module*

### Loupe view

Loupe view is useful because it allows you to preview and magnify your photos in unique ways. For example, clicking a photo in Loupe view magnifies it to a 1:1 ratio. Clicking again fits the photo to the center pane again. You can also change magnification by clicking one of the magnification settings in the upper-right corner of the Navigator panel, shown in Exhibit 1-13. The Navigator panel is located at the top of the left panel group.

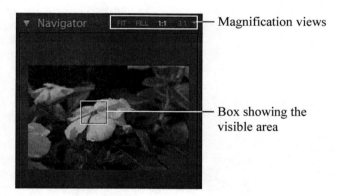

— Magnification views

— Box showing the
visible area

*Exhibit 1-13: Magnification views in the Navigator panel*

When you're viewing a magnified photo, parts of the photo will likely expand outside the boundaries of the center pane. You can shift the visible area by either dragging in the center pane, or by dragging the small box in the Navigator panel. The area inside the box shows the area of the photo visible in the center pane. You can also switch between Grid view and Loupe view by double-clicking a photo in the grid.

### Temporarily zooming and dragging

If you are viewing a photo in Loupe view with the Fit magnification selected, you can also temporarily zoom in and out of photos by clicking and holding the mouse button. When you do, the photo temporarily switches to 1:1 magnification. If you drag while holding the mouse button, you can scroll to view other areas of the photo. When you release the mouse button, the photo returns to its previous magnification.

### Compare and Survey views

In Compare view, you can magnify and compare two specific photos in the library. To use this view, you need to first select two photos in Grid view. When you switch to Compare view, only the two photos you selected are visible. In Survey view, you can view and compare three or more photos.

### Selecting multiple photos

You can select multiple photos in Grid view by holding Ctrl or Shift and clicking the photos you want. Pressing Ctrl allows you to select non-continuous photos. Pressing Shift allows you to select a range.

*Do it!*

## C-1: Viewing photos in the Library

| Here's how | Here's why |
|---|---|
| 1 In the Library panel, click **All Photographs** | (You'll need to scroll up to view the Library panel.) To display all photos you've imported. |
| 2 Observe the photos in the grid | Currently, only index numbers are visible in the upper-left corner above each photo. |
| 3 Press ⬚J⬚ | Now there is more information visible for each photo, including the file name, the file type, and the photo dimensions. |
| Press ⬚J⬚ again | Now all photo information is removed, including the index numbers. |
| Press ⬚J⬚ again | Now the index numbers are visible again. You'll make the size of the photos in the Grid smaller so that there are more photos per row. |
| 4 Click the triangle to the right of the Grid view options | To display the list. |
| Click **Painter** | <br><br>To hide the Painter icon. |

5  In the toolbar, drag the
   Thumbnails slider to the left

Until there is an extra photo per row.

6  In the Grid, click photo 33

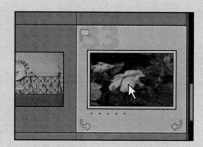

To select the photo of a white flower. (You'll
need to scroll down in the library to see the
photo.) When you select it, a preview appears in
the Navigator panel.

   Observe the Filmstrip

Even without photo information visible in the
Grid, you can view the file name for a selected
photo in the information at the top of the
Filmstrip. Photo 33 is DSC_0582.NEF.

7  In the toolbar at the bottom of the
   center pane, click the Loupe View
   button as shown

To display the selected photo in Loupe view.

8  In the left panel group, in the
   Navigator panel, click **Fill**

To change the magnification.

9  In the center pane, click once on
   the photo

To view it at 1:1 view, in which each pixel of
your monitor corresponds to one pixel in the
photo. This view accurately represents the detail
present in the photo.

10 In the Navigator panel, drag the square

To change the portion of the photo visible in the center panel.

In the center pane, click the photo again.

To return to Fill view.

11 In the Navigator panel, click **Fit**

To return to Fit view.

12 In the toolbar, click the Grid View button as shown

To return to Grid view. You'll now display two photos in Compare view.

13 Hold down (CTRL) and click photo 34

To select it at the same time as photo 33. (Both are similar photos of white flowers.)

14 In the toolbar, click the Compare View button as shown

To display the two selected photos in Compare view. At their current size, you can't really see many differences. You'll enlarge the photos to see them better.

15 In the toolbar, drag the Zoom slider slightly to the right

To increase the magnification to Fill.

16 Drag one of the photos to the left or right

To change what is visible. Dragging one version automatically repositions the other. At this size, you can see a slight difference in the two photos—the background of the right one is slightly blurrier.

17 In the toolbar, drag the Zoom slider to the right

To increase the magnification to 1:1.

Reposition the photos so that the water droplets on the petals are visible

(If necessary.) At this size you can see the details in the photos much clearer. The water droplets are sharper overall in the left photo.

| 18 | In the toolbar, click the Loupe View button | To switch back to Loupe view. |
|---|---|---|
| 19 | Return to the Fit view | |

20 In the Filmstrip, click the third photo of the white flowers

(The photo is just to the right of the currently selected photos.) To deselect the prior selected photos and display this one. You'll now explore ways to temporarily magnify photos.

| 21 | In the center pane, hold the mouse button down on one of the flowers' leaves | To temporarily zoom on that photo area. |
|---|---|---|
| | Release the mouse button | To return to Fit view. |
| | Temporarily zoom in on a few more places in the photo | Hold down the mouse button on those areas. |
| 22 | Hold down the mouse button and drag within the preview | To temporarily zoom and pan the photo. |
| | Release the mouse button | To return to Fit view. |
| 23 | Return to Grid view | In the toolbar, click the Grid View button. |

## The Quick Develop panel

*Explanation*

Although most photo adjustments are performed in the Develop module, you can make quick adjustments in the Library module by using the Quick Develop panel in the right panel group. The panel, shown in Exhibit 1-14, contains basic options for making color and tone adjustments. Many options in the panel have arrows to the left and right. Clicking the single or double arrows makes adjustments in smaller or larger increments. Also, several options have arrows to the right of them. Click these arrows to expand that section and view more options.

Keep in mind that any adjustments you make in Lightroom are non-destructive to your photos. So, for example, if you adjust photo exposure, the results are visible only in Lightroom. Should you open the photo in another application, it will be exactly as it was when you downloaded it from your camera.

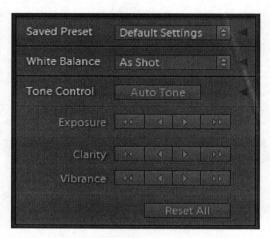

*Exhibit 1-14: The Quick Develop panel*

### Resetting photos

Often, you'll experiment with the settings in the Quick Develop panel, and then perhaps want to undo the changes. You can quickly reset a photo to its import settings by clicking Reset All in the bottom-right corner of the panel. You can also undo individual settings by clicking the setting name. For example, click Exposure to reset the photo to its original exposure.

### Rotating photos

In Grid view, there are several techniques you can use to rotate photos.

- When you point to a photo, rotate icons appear in the lower-left and right corners, as shown in Exhibit 1-15. To rotate a photo, click the rotate icon representing the direction you want to rotate it.
- Select the photo(s) you want to rotate and choose Photo, Rotate Left or Rotate Right.
- To rotate a photo(s) clockwise, press Ctrl+]. To rotate a photo(s) counter-clockwise, press Ctrl+[.

Rotate icons

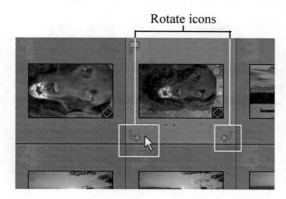

*Exhibit 1-15: An example of rotating a photo*

*Do it!*

## C-2: Performing basic photo adjustments

| Here's how | Here's why |
|---|---|
| 1 In the Grid, select photos 1 and 2 | (Click photo 1, hold down Ctrl, and click photo 2.) To select the two black Labrador photos. |
| 2 Point to the first photo | When you point to the photo, rotate icons appear in the lower-left and right corners. |
| Click as shown | <br>To rotate both selected photos counter-clockwise. |
| 3 Hold down ( CTRL ) and click photo 2 | To deselect it, leaving only photo 1 selected. |
| 4 In the right panel group, in the Quick Develop panel, to the left of Exposure, click as shown | <br>To darken the exposure 1/3 of an f-stop. |
| Click as shown | <br>To darken the exposure a full f-stop. The adjustment is more apparent in the Navigator panel preview. |
| 5 To the right of Exposure, click as shown | <br>To expand the panel section and view more adjustment options. |
| 6 To the right of Contrast, click as shown | <br>To increase the contrast. |

# Topic D: The Lightroom interface

*Explanation*

Lightroom is designed to help photographers view and adjust their photos, and this includes making it quick and easy to manipulate and hide interface elements that get in the way.

## Manipulating interface elements

Depending on the size of your monitor, your photos might appear small even in Loupe or Compare views. You can quickly hide interface elements by collapsing panel groups or by using several quick keyboard shortcuts.

If you study the Lightroom interface, you'll notice four small triangles, one at each edge of the interface (shown in Exhibit 1-16). Clicking these triangles collapses and expands the panel groups or interface elements. For example, if you click the right-most triangle, you'll collapse the right panel group. Each time you collapse a panel group or interface element, the center pane expands, giving you a larger preview. To expand the interface elements, click again on the triangles.

If an interface element is collapsed, you can also temporarily expand it by pointing to the small triangle. When you move away from the triangle, the interface element will collapse again.

*Exhibit 1-16: Collapsing/expanding interface elements*

### Screen and Lights Out modes

You can make broad adjustments to interface elements by using commands in the Windows menu. Using the Screen mode submenu, you can view the interface in either Standard or Fullscreen mode. Standard mode operates like other Windows applications. You can minimize or maximize the application by using the Windows toolbar, or quit the application by clicking the close button. In Fullscreen mode, the interface expands to the full width of the monitor window, and only the main menu is visible. The Lights Out submenu provides choices that either dim or blacken all interface elements, which makes it easier for you to clearly see your photos without any surrounding interface distractions.

### Basic keyboard shortcuts

You can also use keyboard shortcuts to quickly show/hide interface elements. All applications offer keyboard shortcuts, but in Lightroom they can dramatically improve your workflow, so it's important to learn and use them. The following table describes the basic interface shortcuts.

| Shortcut | Description |
| --- | --- |
| Tab | Collapses/expands both the left and right panel groups. |
| Shift+Tab | Collapses/expands all four interface elements surrounding the center pane. |
| F key | Switches between Standard screen mode and Fullscreen with Menu mode. |
| L key | Rotates through Lights modes (Lights On, Lights Dim, Lights Out). |

### Manipulating panels

Sometimes the panels within the left and right panel groups can be difficult to work with if they are all expanded. For example, in the left panel group, when the Navigator panel is visible, you'll likely need to scroll up and down in the Folders panel in order to scan through your list of folders. To make things easier, you can collapse and expand individual panels. When you collapse a panel, the remaining panels are more clearly visible. To collapse/expand a panel, click the panel title.

You can resize the width of panel groups. This is especially useful when using the Folders panel if your folder titles are longer than the current panel width. When this occurs, the folder titles get cut off, which can make it difficult to identify them. To expand the width of a panel group, point to the left or right edge until two arrows appear pointing in opposite directions, as shown in Exhibit 1-17. With the arrows visible, drag to the left or right.

*Exhibit 1-17: Resizing a panel group*

*Do it!*

## D-1: Adjusting interface elements

| Here's how | Here's why |
|---|---|
| 1 In the left panel group, in the Folders panel, expand Prior shoots | (If necessary.) (Click the small triangle to the left of Prior shoots.) The more folders visible in the panel, the more you'll have to scroll to see them. To make the folders more visible, you'll collapse the Navigator panel. |
| 2 Click the Navigator panel title | To collapse it. In the Folders panel, the longer folder names are being cut off. You'll resize the left panel group to make it entirely visible. |
| 3 Point to the right edge of the panel group | Until two arrows appear pointing in opposite directions. |
| With the arrows visible, drag the edge to the right as shown | (Until the entire folder names are visible.) The Grid decreases in size. You'll return the panel group to its original width. |
| 4 Drag the right edge of the panel group to the left | Until it won't go any further. You can decrease the width of the panel group only a certain amount. |
| 5 In the grid, locate photo 27 | The photo of the arctic fox. |
| Double-click the photo | To view it in Loupe view. You'd like it to appear larger so you can see more details. |
| 6 On the left side of the interface, click the small triangle, as shown | To hide the left panel group. The photo enlarges to fill the space formerly occupied by the panel. |
| 7 Click the small triangle on the right side of the interface | To collapse the right panel group. You decide to apply an adjustment. You'll do this by temporarily showing the right panel group. |

| | | |
|---|---|---|
| 8 | Point to the small triangle on the right side of the interface. | To make the right panel group expand temporarily, covering the right side of the photo. |
| | Click twice, as shown | |
| | | To brighten the photo. |
| 9 | Move the pointer away from the panel group | After a few moments, the right panel group collapses again, uncovering the photo. |
| 10 | Click the small triangle on the right side of the interface again | To expand the panel group again. |
| | Expand the left panel group | Click the small triangle on the left side of the interface. You'll now experiment with basic keyboard interface shortcuts. |
| 11 | Press (TAB) | To collapse the left and right panel groups. |
| | Press (TAB) again | To expand the panel groups. |
| 12 | Press (SHIFT) + (TAB) | To collapse all four interface elements surrounding the center pane. |
| | Press (F) | To switch to Fullscreen with Menu mode. (The minimize, maximize, and exit buttons in the upper-right corner of the application are no longer available.) |
| | Press (SHIFT) + (TAB) again | To display all four panels. |
| 13 | Press (L) | To enter Lights Dim mode. |
| | Press (L) again | To enter Lights Out mode. |
| | Press (L) again | To enter Lights On mode again. |

## Navigation shortcuts

As mentioned earlier, keyboard shortcuts are a big part of Lightroom. The application is designed to streamline your workflow, and keyboard shortcuts can significantly improve your efficiency. The following table provides some of the more commonly used shortcuts you can use to navigate modules, views, and photos.

| Shortcut | Description |
|---|---|
| Ctrl+Alt+1, 2, 3, 4, or 5 | Switches between modules: Library (1), Develop (2), Slideshow (3), Print (4), and Web (5). |
| Ctrl+Alt+Up Arrow | Returns to previous module. |
| G | Switches to Grid view. |
| E | Switches to Loupe view. |
| C | Switches to Compare view. |
| ` | Toggles between Loupe view and the previous view. |
| Left and right arrow keys | Selects the photo to the left or right of the currently selected photo. |
| Shift+left or right arrow keys | Selects the photo to the left or right in addition to the currently selected photo. |
| Ctrl+= | Zooms to the next higher magnification. |
| Ctrl+- | Zooms to the next lower magnification. |
| Z | Toggles between 1:1 magnification and the previous magnification. |
| Ctrl+D | Deselects all photos in the library. |
| Shift+Ctrl+D | Deselects all photos except the active photo. |
| Ctrl+Q | Exits the application. |

**Active photos**

In Lightroom, the first photo you select in a group is considered the active photo. You can tell which photo is active because it looks slightly lighter in color than the other selected photos, as shown in Exhibit 1-18. This is helpful if you've been working with a group of photos, but can't remember which one you selected first.

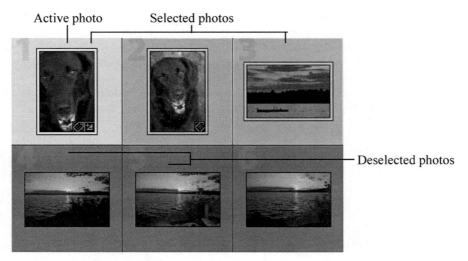

*Exhibit 1-18: The active photo in a group of selected photos*

*Do it!*

### D-2: Navigating by using shortcuts

| Here's how | Here's why |
|---|---|
| 1 Press (CTRL) + (ALT) + (2) | To enter the Develop module. The shortcut for each module is Ctrl plus a number. |
| Press (CTRL) + (ALT) + (3) | To enter the Slideshow module. |
| Press (CTRL) + (ALT) + (4) | To enter the Print module. |
| Press (CTRL) + (ALT) + (5) | To enter the Web module. |
| Press (CTRL) + (ALT) + (1) | To return to the Library module. |
| 2 Press (CTRL) + (ALT) + (↑) | To return to the previous module (in this case, Web). |
| 3 Press (G) | To display photos in Grid view. |
| Press (E) | To display the selected photo in Loupe view. |
| Press (') | To toggle between Loupe and the prior view (in this case, to return to Grid view). |
| 4 Press (→) several times | To navigate to the right in the Filmstrip and the photos in the grid. |
| Press (←) several times | To navigate to the left. |

| | |
|---|---|
| 5  Select photo 60 | The photo of a white bird flying on a beach. |
| Hold (SHIFT) and press (→) | To select the next photo to the right in addition to the selected one. |
| 6  Press (C) | To display the selected photos in Compare view. |
| 7  Press (Z) | To zoom the selected photo to 1:1 magnification. It automatically switches to Loupe view. |
| If necessary, drag the photo to center the bird in the window | |
| Press (C) | To exit Compare view. |
| 8  Press (→) | To view the next photo. |
| If necessary, drag the photo to center the bird in the window | |
| Press (←) and (→) repeatedly to quickly alternate between the two bird photos to compare them, stopping on the one you prefer more | |
| 9  Press (CTRL) + (–) | To zoom in to the next lower level of magnification. |
| Press (CTRL) + (=) | To zoom back in. |
| Press (CTRL) + (–) twice | To zoom back further. |
| 10  Press (G) | To return to Grid view. |
| Press (CTRL) + (D) | To deselect all photos. |
| 11  Press (CTRL) + (Q) | To exit Lightroom. |

# Unit summary: Getting started

**Topic A**     In this topic, you explored the basics of the Lightroom interface, common workflow techniques, and discussed the differences between working with **JPEGs** and **Camera RAW** files.

**Topic B**     In this topic, you imported photos and set a variety of import options. You controlled the way photos are organized in the Folders panel, and you imported photos with **metadata** information and **develop settings** applied to them.

**Topic C**     In this topic, you adjusted the way photos are viewed in Lightroom. You changed the way **the grid** shows photos, switched between Grid, Loupe, Compare, and Survey view modes, and you learned how to zoom in and out of photos and make basic adjustments.

**Topic D**     In this topic, you learned how to manipulate the Lightroom interface, and you used **keyboard shortcuts** to improve efficiency. You learned how to collapse and expand panel groups and panels, and you used shortcuts to switch modules, select photos, increase/decrease magnification, and activate various Light modes.

## Independent practice activity

In this activity, you'll import a folder of photos with specific metadata and develop settings applied. You'll also view photos in the library by using several views, and you'll manipulate interface elements by using keyboard shortcuts.

1  Start Lightroom.

2  Import the photo in the 2006-07-03 River folder with the following settings:
   - Reference file in its existing location.
   - Apply the My copyright metadata preset.

   (*Hint:* At the bottom of the left panel group, click Import. The folder is located in the Media subfolder in the Student Data folder. Also, be sure to remove the Grayscale Conversion develop setting you applied to the last photos you imported.)

3  View all the photos in the library. (*Hint:* In the Library panel, click All Photographs.)

4  Select photo 42 (one of the Yellow Labrador photos).

5  View the photo in Loupe view. (*Hint:* In the toolbar, click the Loupe View button or press E.)

6  Expand the Navigator panel and magnify the photo to 1:1 magnification. (*Hint:* Click the panel title to expand it. In the magnification settings on the top of the panel title bar, click 1:1.)

7  Use the Navigator panel to view a different area of the photo. (*Hint:* Drag the box in the Navigator panel.)

8  Switch back to Fit magnification. (*Hint:* In the Navigator panel, click Fit.)

9  Temporarily zoom in on the photo. (*Hint:* Point to an area of the photo, then press and hold the mouse button.)

10  Switch back to Grid view. (*Hint:* Press G.)

11  Add photo 43 to the selection. (*Hint:* Press Ctrl and click photo 43.)

12 Switch to Compare view. (*Hint:* In the toolbar, click the Compare View button or press C.)

13 Switch back to Grid view.

14 Use shortcuts to hide various interface elements. (*Hint:* Experiment with the Tab and L keys.)

15 Exit Lightroom. (*Hint:* Press Ctrl+Q.)

## Review questions

1 Which format is typically best for working with digital photos?

  A  TIFF

  B  JPEG

  C  Camera RAW

  D  GIF

2 Which are modules in Lightroom? (Choose all that apply.)

  A  Library

  B  Develop

  C  Web

  D  Color

3 True or false? When you import photos, you can instruct Lightroom to either move them to a new location or keep them within an existing folder structure.

4 In Loupe view, how do you magnify a photo? (Choose all that apply.)

  A  In the Navigator panel, click a magnification preset.

  B  Press and hold the mouse button on a portion of the photo in the center pane.

  C  In the toolbar, click a magnification preset.

  D  Click the photo in the center pane.

5 Which keyboard shortcut collapses the left and right panel groups?

  A  Shift

  B  G

  C  L

  D  Tab

# Unit 2
## The library

**Unit time: 60 minutes**

Complete this unit, and you'll know how to:

**A** Flag, rate, stack, and sort photos, and cull photos by using Survey view.

**B** Create and manipulate keywords, create collections, and filter photos in Grid view.

**C** Synchronize develop settings and metadata adjustments within groups of photos.

**D** Export photos in different formats.

# Topic A:  Sorting photos

*Explanation*

After you've imported photos, you'll likely preview and select the ones you like better than the others. You can do this by flagging them, applying a rating system, and by previewing similar photos in Survey view.

## Flag photos

To flag photos:

1    In the Grid, select the photos you want to flag.

2    Do one of the following:

- In the Grid, point to one of the selected photos. When you do, a small flag icon appears in the upper-left corner as shown in Exhibit 2-1. Click the flag icon to flag all the selected photos. Using this method, you can apply only the Pick flag.

- In the toolbar, click the flag type you want. You can flag photos as "picked" or flag them as "rejected." (*Note:* To flag photos by using the toolbar, you'll first need to show the Pick options. See "Adding options to the toolbar" below.)

- Choose Photo, Set Flag and then choose the flag you want.

*Exhibit 2-1: Flagging a photo by using the Grid*

### Adding options to the toolbar

By default, the toolbar shows a default set of options only for the module you're working in. You can add more options to the toolbar by selecting them from the toolbar list, shown in Exhibit 2-2.

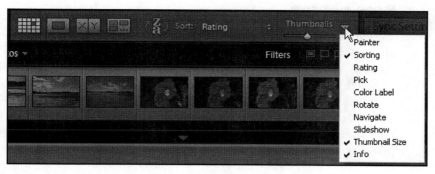

*Exhibit 2-2: Adding options to the Library toolbar*

*Do it!*

## A-1:   Flagging photos

| Here's how | Here's why |
|---|---|
| 1  Start Lightroom | |
| 2  Press (G) | (If necessary.) To display the photos in Grid view in the Library module. |
| 3  Press (CTRL) + (D) | (If necessary.) To deselect any photos. To make selecting photos easier, you'll hide the left and right panel groups. |
| 4  Press (TAB) | To hide the panel groups. |
| 5  Scroll up to view the beginning of the library | (If necessary.) You're putting together a portfolio of candid family photos, and you want to flag photos you might want to include. |
| 6  Ctrl-click the first two photos | (The two photos of the black Labrador.) To select them. |
| 7  Include the following photos in the selection:<br><br>18, 19, 20, 21, 22, and 24 | Be sure to hold Ctrl as you click the photos to include them in the selection. |
| 8  Point to one of the selected photos | When you point to the photo, a small flag icon appears in the upper-left corner. |
| 9  Click the flag icon | To flag all the selected photos as "picks." |

## Rate photos

*Explanation*

You've learned that when you point to a photo in the Grid, certain adjustment options appear, such as rotation or flag icons. Included are a series of five small dots at the bottom. These dots represent a rating system you can use to filter the photos on a scale of zero to five stars; zero stars being the lowest, and five stars being the highest. When you click one of the dots, stars appear starting with the leftmost dot and ending on the dot you clicked. For example, if you click the third dot, three stars appear as shown in the example in Exhibit 2-3. You can also rank photos by selecting a photo and then pressing 1 through 5 on the keyboard.

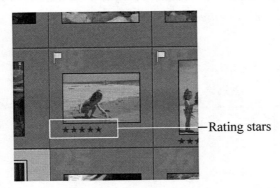

*Exhibit 2-3: A photo showing a rating of five stars*

### Sort photos

After you've flagged and rated photos, you can sort them in the Grid by choosing Pick or Rating from the Sort list in the toolbar. If you select Rating, the Grid moves the photos you rated to the front of the index order based on their rating. The highest rated photos are first. Following the rated photos, the remaining photos appear in reverse chronological order. If you select Pick, the photos you flagged are moved to the beginning of the library.

You can filter photos in a similar way in the Filmstrip. To filter flagged photos, select a flag icon in the Filters section, shown in Exhibit 2-4. To filter photos based on rating, set the rating level you want. If you filter photos by using the Filmstrip, the photos that aren't rated or flagged in the library are hidden.

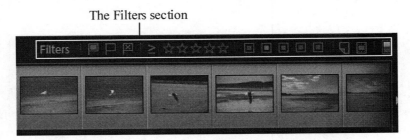

*Exhibit 2-4: The Filters section in the Filmstrip*

*Do it!*

## A-2:   Rating and sorting photos

| Here's how | Here's why |
|---|---|
| 1  Scroll to the top of the library | If necessary. |
| 2  Press ⌷CTRL⌷ + ⌷D⌷ | To deselect the photos. |
| 3  Point to the first photo | |
| | A row of five dots is visible beneath the photo. |
|    Click the third dot | |
| | To assign a rating of three stars. You can also assign ratings by typing a number. |
| 4  Select photo 2 | |
|    Type **4** | To assign a rating of four stars. |
| 5  Assign the following ratings: | You'll now sort the photos according to their rating rather than by the date the photos were taken. |
|    Photo 18: 5 stars | |
|    Photo 19: 4 stars | |
|    Photo 20: 5 stars | |
|    Photo 21: 4 stars | |
|    Photo 22: 2 stars | |
|    Photo 24: 4 stars | |

6 In the toolbar, from the Sort list, choose **Rating**

All the rated photos appear at the beginning of the library based on their ratings. Following the rated photos, the remaining photos appear in reverse chronological order.

7 In the toolbar, from the Sort list, choose **Capture Time**

To view the photos based on their capture time again.

8 In the Filmstrip, in the Filter section, click the Pick flag icon, as shown

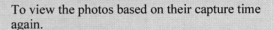

Now only the flagged photos are visible. All unflagged photos in the library are hidden.

9 In the Filmstrip, click the Pick flag icon again

To show all the photos in the library again.

10 Click the greater than or equal to sign and choose **Rating is equal to**

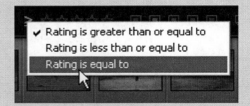

11 In the Filmstrip, click the third dot, as shown

Now only the photo rated with three stars is visible.

12 Click the second star

To lower the rating filter. Now only the photo rated with two stars is visible.

## Stack photos

*Explanation*

Sometimes you might have a group of photos that are very similar. For example, you might have taken a series of photos using an auto-bracket feature on your camera. When you have photos that are almost identical, they can be hard to manage, especially in a large library. To make things easier, you can stack groups of photos instead of having them scattered across rows of thumbnails.

To stack photos:

1  In Grid view, select the photos you want to combine in a stack.
2  Choose Photo, Stacking, Group into Stack. You can also press Ctrl+G.

Photos are stacked based on their sort order in the Grid, with the active photo on top. You can identify stacked photos by a small badge in the upper-left corner, as shown in Exhibit 2-5. The number on the badge indicates the number of photos in the stack. After you've stacked photos, you can expand and collapse the stack by clicking the badge. You can also unstack photos by choosing Photo, Stacking, Unstack.

Stack badge

*Exhibit 2-5: An example of stacked photos*

### Turning off the Filters section in the Filmstrip

You can keep the filter settings you've applied in the Filmstrip but temporarily see all the photos in the library. The Filters section is unique because you can also turn it off and on without having to undo any settings. To do this, click the small switch on the right side, as shown in Exhibit 2-6.

The On/Off switch

*Exhibit 2-6: The On/Off switch in the Filmstrip*

*Do it!*

## A-3: Stacking photos

| Here's how | Here's why |
|---|---|
| 1 In the Filmstrip, in the Filters section, click the On/Off switch | To turn off the filter settings. All the photos in the library are visible again. |
| 2 In the Grid, select photos 13 through 17 | (Press Ctrl or Shift and click the photos.) (The photos should all be similar waterfall photos. If the numbering is off, select the waterfall photos.) These photos are all very similar, so you'll stack them. |
| 3 Choose **Photo**, **Stacking**, **Group into Stack** |

Only the active photo is still visible, and it shows a stack badge in the upper-left corner indicating there are five photos in the stack. |
| 4 Click the badge icon | To expand the stack. The hidden photos are visible again. |
| 5 Point to the second photo in the stack | When you point to the photo, a badge appears indicating it is 2 of 5. |
| 6 Click the badge icon in the first photo | To collapse the stack again. |

## Survey view

*Explanation*

You'll likely want to compare groups of photos that are similar so that you can choose the best of a series. You can use Survey view to do this quickly. To compare photos, select the photos you want to compare; then switch to Survey view by clicking the Survey view button at the bottom of the center pane, or by pressing N.

When you're viewing photos in Survey view, you can add or remove photos by:

- Pressing Ctrl and selecting or deselecting them in the Filmstrip.
- Pressing Ctrl and clicking the photo.
- Clicking the small "x" in the lower-right corner of the photo.

### Deleting photos

To delete photos, select the photo you want to remove and press Backspace or Delete. When you do, the Confirm dialog box appears as shown in Exhibit 2-7, asking if you want to delete the photo from the disk, or just remove it from Lightroom. To delete the photo from Lightroom, click Remove. This removes the photo from the library, but leaves it in the folder from which you imported it. To remove the photo from the library and move it to the recycle bin on your computer, click Delete from Disk.

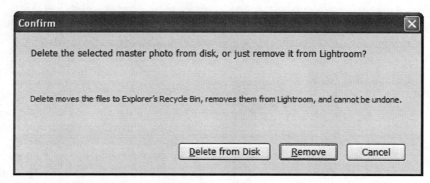

*Exhibit 2-7: The Confirm dialog box*

*Do it!*

### A-4: Culling by using Survey view

| Here's how | Here's why |
|---|---|
| 1 On the waterfall photo, click the badge icon | To expand the stack of photos. The photos are selected automatically. |
| | The photos are all similar, so you'll preview them in Survey view, and remove the ones you don't want. |
| 2 Press (N) | To view the photos in Survey view. The left-most photo was taken by using a faster shutter speed, so the water is clearer. You want to keep two versions, the clear photo and one in which the motion of the water is more blurred. Because you know you'll keep the clear version, you'll remove it from Survey view. |
| 3 In the lower-right corner of the clear photo, click the "×" | |
| | To remove it. The photo is deselected and no longer visible in Survey view. However, it is still visible in the Filmstrip. |
| | Of the four remaining photos, the right-most photo has a nice misty effect for the water. You'll keep that photo and remove the prior three. You want to remove the three photos from the library. |
| 4 Click photo DSC_4322 | To select it. |
| Press (← BACKSPACE) | A dialog box appears asking if you want to remove the photo from Lightroom, or delete it completely from your computer. You'd prefer to keep it in the folder from which you imported it. |
| 5 Click **Remove** | This time, the photo is no longer included in the Filmstrip. The center pane returns to Grid view. |
| 6 Remove the photos DSC_4323 and DSC_4324 from the library | (DSC_4323 and DSC_4324.) Click to select the photo, and press Backspace. In the dialog box, click Remove. (Be sure to keep photo DSC_4325.) |
| 7 Collapse the stack | Click the stacking badge in the first image of the stack. |

# Topic B:  Organizing photos

*Explanation*

In addition to assigning metadata to photos as you import them, you can add metadata after photos are imported. You can use metadata to organize and track your photos. You can also organize photos by creating collections or by filtering them based on certain criteria.

## Keywords

If you assigned keywords to photos as you imported them, the information will be visible for the selected photos in the Keywording and Metadata panels (in the right panel group). You can quickly tell which photos have keywords applied to them by the presence of a small badge in the lower-right corner, as shown in Exhibit 2-8.

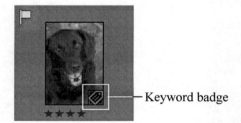

*Exhibit 2-8: A photo thumbnail with a keyword badge*

Sometimes you might want to apply the same keywords to other photos in the library. You can do this by using the Keyword Tags panel in the left panel group, shown in Exhibit 2-9. The difference between the *Keyword Tags* panel and the *Keywording* panel is that the Keyword Tags panel shows all keywords used in the library as well as the number of photos with the keywords applied to them. The Keywording panel shows only the keywords applied to the photos currently selected.

*Exhibit 2-9: The Keywords panel*

You can apply keywords to other photos by dragging the photos directly to the keywords in the Keyword Tags panel list. You can also use the keywords in the panel to view specific photos. For example, to view only the photos with the Dogs keyword applied, click the keyword in the list.

**The Metadata Browser**

You can view photos by using the Metadata Browser panel. The panel shows basic metadata generated by the camera you shot the pictures with, as well as some that you specified when importing the photos. For example, if wanted to view photos shot on a specific date, you could do so by expanding the dates in the Date section, as shown in Exhibit 2-10.

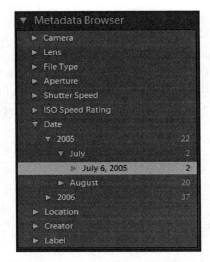

*Exhibit 2-10: The Metadata Browser panel*

*Do it!*

## B-1: Assigning keywords

| Here's how | Here's why |
|---|---|
| 1 Select the second of two photos of a black Labrador | The photo thumbnail has a small keyword badge in the lower-right corner, indicating it has keyword(s) applied to it. |
| 2 Press TAB | To show the left and right panel groups. |
| 3 Collapse the Navigator panel | (If necessary.) To collapse the panel, click the panel title. |
| 4 In the right panel group, scroll down to view the Keywording panel | (If necessary.) This photo has the keywords Animals and Dogs applied. |
| 5 In the left panel group, scroll down to view the Keyword Tags panel | ▼ Keyword Tags +<br>✓ Animals 2<br>✓ Dogs 2<br><br>The panel shows the same keywords, and indicates that two photos in the library have the keywords applied to them. Also, the checkmarks on the left indicate the selected photo has the keywords applied. |
| 6 Press ← | The first Labrador photo has the same keywords applied. |

7 Select the series of wildlife photos near the middle of the library

You'll apply the Animal keyword to the selected photos.

Drag one of the selected photos to the keyword Animals in the Keyword Tags panel

The number to the right of the Animals keyword changes, and the selected photos in the Grid now show keyword badges.

8 Select the series of photos of the Yellow Labrador

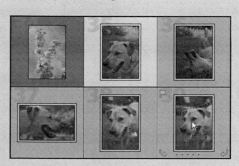

9 Apply both the Animals and Dogs keywords to the selected photos

Drag one of the selected photos to both keywords.

10 In the Keyword Tags panel, click the **Animals** keyword

In the Grid, only photos with the Animal keyword applied are visible.

Click the **Dogs** keyword

Only photos with the Dogs keyword applied are visible.

11 In the Library panel, click **All Photographs**

(If necessary.) To display all photos.

## Manipulate keywords

*Explanation*    In addition to applying existing keywords, you can create new keywords. As the keywords list grows, you can nest keywords to manage them.

To create new keywords:

1   Select the photos for which you want to create a new keyword.

2   Click the small plus sign on the right side of the Keyword Tags panel title bar. When you do, the Create Keyword Tag dialog box appears, as shown in Exhibit 2-11.

3   In the Keyword Tag box, enter the keyword you want to add.

4   In the Synonyms box, enter any synonyms for the keyword. Synonyms appear in the Implied Keywords section in the Keywording panel.

5   If you want to automatically apply the new keyword to the selected photos, check Include selected photos. You can also set exporting options.

6   Click Create.

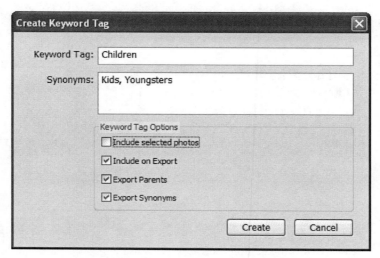

*Exhibit 2-11: The Create Keyword Tag dialog box*

You can also create and apply keywords by selecting photos in the Grid and entering the keywords you want in the Keywording panel. If you use this method, you cannot specify synonyms or other options for keywords like you can in the Create Keyword tag dialog box.

### Nesting keywords

You can nest keywords under other similar ones. For example, because dogs are animals, you could nest the Dogs keyword under Animals, thus simplifying the list, as shown in Exhibit 2-12. To nest keywords, drag them in the list to the keyword you want to nest them under.

*Exhibit 2-12: An example of a nested keyword*

You can nest keywords as you create them. To do this, select a keyword in the list before you click the plus sign in the Keyword Tags panel title bar. The new keyword will be nested under the keyword you selected.

### Removing keywords

To remove keywords from the library, select the keyword in the Keyword Tags panel, then click the small minus sign on the right side of the panel title bar. When you do, a dialog box appears asking if you're sure you want to delete the keyword. If you delete the keyword, it is automatically removed from all photos in the library to which it was applied.

### Removing keywords from specific photos

To remove keywords from photos, you need to use the Keywording panel, shown in Exhibit 2-13. Select the photo (or photos) from which you want to remove a keyword. In the Keywording panel, select the keyword and press Backspace to remove it.

*Exhibit 2-13: Removing a keyword by using the Applied Keywords panel*

### Keyword sets

If you have a large collection of keywords, you can further organize them by creating *Keyword Sets*. For example, you can create keyword sets with keyword tags for certain events, locations, people, or assignments. To create a keyword set, choose Save as New Preset from the Set list in the Keywording panel.

*Do it!*

## B-2: Manipulating keywords

| Here's how | Here's why |
|---|---|
| 1 Select the series of children photos | |
| | (The photos should be in the 14–20 range.) |
| | You'll create a new keyword for these photos. |
| 2 Click + on the right of the Keyword Tags panel title bar | |
| | The Create Keyword Tag dialog box appears. |
| 3 In the Keyword Tag box, enter **Children** | |
| In the Synonyms box, enter **Kids, Youngsters** | Be sure to separate the synonyms with a comma. |
| 4 Under Keyword Tag Options, check **Include selected photos** | |
| 5 Click **Create** | The new keyword is selected automatically in the Keyword Tags panel, so only those photos are visible in the grid. |
| 6 In the right panel group, observe the Keywording panel | The new keyword is visible under Keyword Tags |
| 7 In the Library panel, click **All Photographs** | |
| 8 Scan through the library and select the photos of people that aren't children | There is a grayscale photo of the restaurateur some band member photos. |

9  Click + on the right of the Keyword Tags panel title bar

To open the Create Keyword Tag dialog box.

10  In the Keyword Tag box, enter **People**

Under Keyword Tag Options, verify that **Include selected photos** is selected

11  Click **Create**

You've now decided to nest the Children keyword under People.

12  In the Keyword Tags panel, drag the Children keyword to People

A triangle appears to the left of People, and the number to the right of People increases to 12, because children are now nested under People. In the library, all the photos of people are visible, including the children photos.

13  Click the triangle to the left of the People keyword

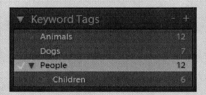

Children now appear nested beneath People.

14  Click the Children keyword

To view only the photos of children.

15  Click the People keyword again

All the photos of people are visible, including the children photos.

## Collections

*Explanation*

You can group photos in order to reference them quickly by using the Collections panel, shown in Exhibit 2-14. Collections are especially useful as a way to group photos that are in different folders. Using collections, you can quickly view specific photos from multiple folders without having to move them between folders or repeatedly select them within the library.

*Exhibit 2-14: The Collections panel*

To create a collection:

1   Select the photos you want to include in the collection.

2   In the Collections panel, on the right side of the title bar, click the small plus sign. The Create Collection dialog box appears, as shown in Exhibit 2-15.

3   In the Collection box, enter a descriptive title for the collection.

4   Check Include selected photos to automatically include the photos you selected. You can also create a collection and add photos to it later by dragging them to the collection title in the panel.

5   Click Create to create the collection.

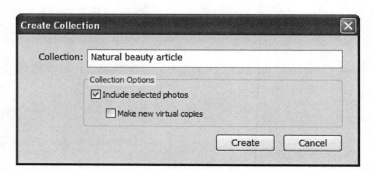

*Exhibit 2-15: The Create Collection dialog box*

*Do it!*          **B-3:   Creating a collection**

| Here's how | Here's why |
|---|---|
| 1  In the Library panel, click **All Photographs** | A magazine editor asked you to gather photos that express natural beauty in broad conceptual ways, which will be used for an article.<br><br>Because this is for a specific project, you'll create a collection to hold these photos. |
| 2  Select photos shown here |  |
| 3  In the left panel group, scroll down to view the Collections panel | (If necessary.) Because there are no collections created yet, the panel is empty. |
| 4  Click + on the right side of the title bar | The Create Collection dialog box appears. |
| 5  In the Collection box, enter **Natural beauty article** | |
| 6  Check **Include selected photos** | |
| Click **Create** | The collection appears in the Collections panel, and only the photos you selected are visible. |

### Quick Collection

*Explanation*

You can create a Quick Collection to quickly group photos for a specific purpose, such as ones you need to adjust in the Develop module, or in preparation for creating a more permanent collection. The Quick Collection is in the Library panel, as shown in Exhibit 2-16.

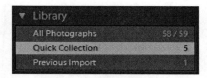

*Exhibit 2-16: The Quick Collection in the Library panel*

To add photos to the Quick Collection, select the photos you want to add, point to one of the selected photos, and click the small dot that appears in the upper-right corner, as shown in Exhibit 2-17. When you click the dot, it darkens, indicating that the photos are part of the Quick Collection. You can also add photos to the Quick Collection by pressing B, dragging one of the selected photos to Quick Collection in the Library panel, or by Choosing Photo, Add to Quick Collection.

*Exhibit 2-17: Adding a photo to the Quick Collection*

To view the Quick Collection, click it in the Library panel. You can also toggle between the Quick Collection and the library by pressing Ctrl+B.

Photos listed in the Quick Collection will remain there until you remove them or exit the application. To clear the Quick Collection, press Shift+Ctrl+B.

*Do it!*

## B-4: Adding photos to a Quick Collection

| Here's how | Here's why |
|---|---|
| 1 In the Library panel, click **All Photographs** | You'll add some photos to the Quick Collection that you want to adjust later in the Develop module. |
| 2 Press (CTRL) + (D) | To deselect all photos. |
| 3 Point to the photo shown and observe the dot that appears near the top-right corner | |
| Click the dot | To add the photo to the Quick Collection. The dot darkens and remains when you move the pointer away from the photo. |
| 4 Scroll down and select the faded photo of two zebras | (The photo should be either 24 or 25 in the library.) This photo appears very washed out because of the lighting and haze in the original scene. |
| Press (B) | To add the photo to the Quick Collection. |
| 5 Press (CTRL) + (B) | To show the Quick Collection. |

### The Find panel

*Explanation*
Another way to search for photos is by filtering them by using options in the Find panel, shown in Exhibit 2-18.

*Exhibit 2-18: The Find panel*

You can use the panel to show only photos that fit certain criteria, such as specific metadata applied to them, the file names, or keywords, as seen in the list shown in Exhibit 2-19.

*Exhibit 2-19: Text find options*

To find photos by using the Find panel:

1 Select a folder or collection to search within. You can also search all photos by clicking All Photographs in the Library panel.

2 At the top of the Find panel, check Text.

3 From the Text list choose the text, file name, or type of metadata you want to search.

4 From the Rule list, choose a range for the text search, such as Contains, Contains All, Doesn't Contain, Starts With, or Ends With.

5 Type the text you want to search for in the search text box. Often you will not need to type entire words. Each letter you type further specifies the photos you're looking for.

To find photos based on their capture date, check Date and specify capture date criteria by using the list or by moving the date range sliders.

*Do it!*

**B-5:    Finding photos**

| Here's how | Here's why |
|---|---|
| 1  In the Library panel, click **All Photographs** | |
| 2  In the Find panel, check **Text** | To activate the section. In many cases you won't have to type an entire list item's name; you need to type only as much of a name as necessary to isolate those photos. |
| 3  In the search text box, enter **chi** | The photos tagged with the Children keyword appear. |
|     In the search text box, change the text to **wild** | Five photos appear based on the text "Wild" appearing in folder names. |
| 4  In the Folders panel, observe the Prior shoots folder | The folders are grayed out, with the exception of the Wildlife folder. (It may take a minute for the list to finish updating.) |
| 5  In the Find panel, in the search text box, change the text to **lake** | This search shows all photos from the 2005-08-02 Lake folder, which includes waterfall shots as well. To restrict the shots to only ones specifically of the Lake, you would have to click the Lake folder in the Folders panel. |

# Topic C: Group photo adjustments

*Explanation*

You might want to make adjustments to groups of photos. For example, you might want to apply the same color correction adjustments from one photo to multiple others, or you might want to add more metadata information to photos.

## Synchronizing photos

Earlier you learned how to make photo adjustments by using the Quick Develop panel. Sometimes you might want to apply the same adjustments to other photos in the library. Instead of selecting photos and manually repeating the adjustments, you can use the Sync Settings command at the bottom of the right panel group.

To synchronize a group of photos:

1 Select the photo containing the adjustments you want to copy.

2 Ctrl or Shift-select the photos you want to synchronize with the same adjustments.

3 At the bottom of the right panel group, click Sync Settings to open the Synchronize Settings dialog box, shown in Exhibit 2-20.

4 Check or clear the options you want to apply and click Synchronize.

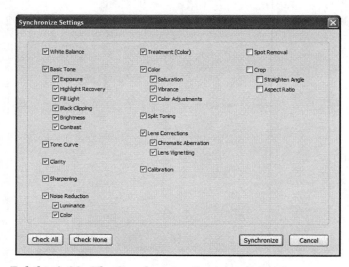

*Exhibit 2-20: The Synchronize Settings dialog box*

*Do it!*

## C-1:   Synchronizing photos

| Here's how | Here's why |
|---|---|
| 1  In the Find panel, in the search text box, change the text to **dogs** | The grid changes to show all the dog photos. You want to work with the yellow Labrador photos. The last two yellow lab photos have good contrast, but the first three have a dull cast to them. |
| 2  Select the yellow Labrador photo shown | |
| 3  In the right panel group, scroll up to view the Quick Develop panel | If necessary. |
| 4  In the panel, to the right of Brightness, click twice as shown | To lighten the photo. |
| 5  In the panel, to the right of Contrast, click the double-arrows | To add some more contrast. |
| 6  In the panel, to the right of Vibrance, click the double-arrows | To increase the vibrance setting.  You think these adjustments might benefit the next two photos. |
| 7  Ctrl-click the other two dark photos of the dog | To add them to the selection. |
| 8  At the bottom of the right panel group, click **Sync Settings** | The Synchronize Settings dialog box appears. You want to apply all the adjustments you made to the first photo, so you'll leave everything checked. |
| 9  Click **Synchronize** | The brightness, contrast, and vibrance adjustments are visible in the photos.  You also want to apply the vibrance adjustment to the first two photos of the black Labrador, but you don't want to include the brightness and contrast adjustments. |
| 10  Ctrl-click black Labrador photos | To add them to the selection. |

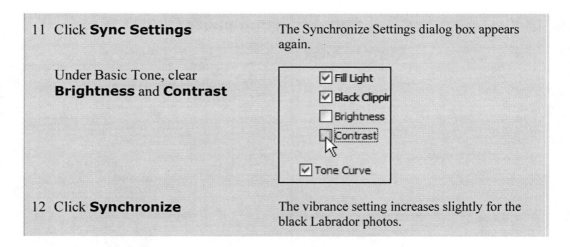

| | |
|---|---|
| 11 Click **Sync Settings** | The Synchronize Settings dialog box appears again. |
| Under Basic Tone, clear **Brightness** and **Contrast** | |
| 12 Click **Synchronize** | The vibrance setting increases slightly for the black Labrador photos. |

## Manipulate metadata

You can make metadata adjustments by using the Metadata panel, shown in Exhibit 2-21. In default view, the panel shows basic camera data and metadata information. You can change the information in the panel by choosing a new view from the list on the right side of the panel title bar. To add or adjust metadata, enter the information you want in the corresponding boxes.

*Exhibit 2-21: The Metadata panel*

There are several ways that you can apply metadata to groups of photos:

- Select the group of photos for which you want to apply the same metadata, then enter the metadata you want in the Metadata panel.

- Select a photo that contains the metadata you want to apply to other photos, and then select other photos for which you want the same metadata applied. At the bottom of the right panel group, click Sync Metadata. When you do, the Synchronize Metadata dialog box appears, as shown in Exhibit 2-22. Check the metadata you want to synchronize and click Synchronize.

- Create a new preset in the Metadata panel. Then select the photos for which you want the same metadata applied and choose the new preset in the panel.

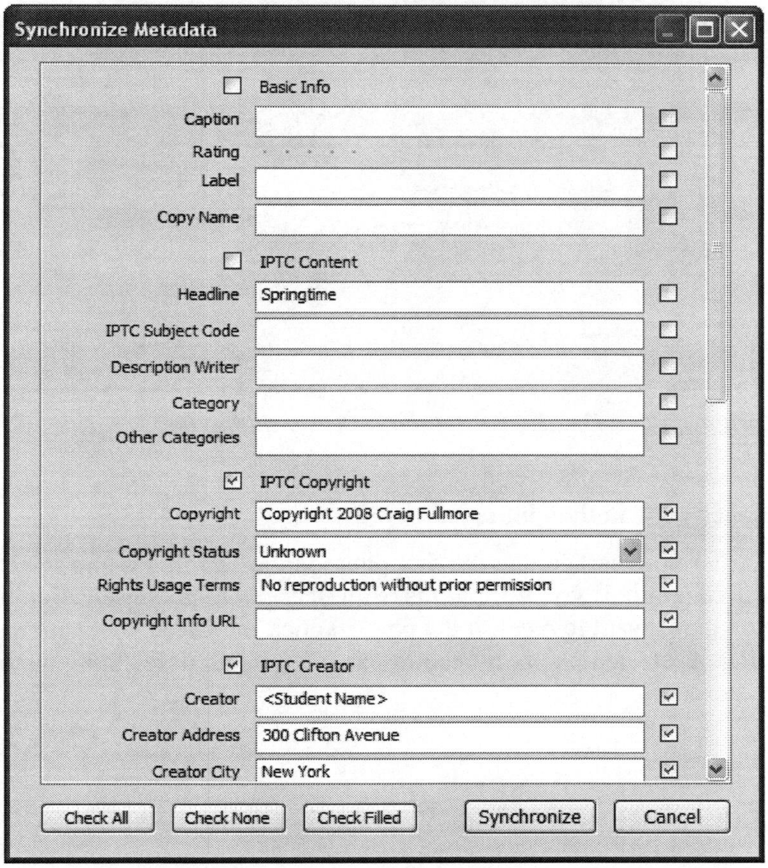

*Exhibit 2-22: The Synchronize Metadata dialog box*

**Presets**

If you want to create a preset in the Metadata panel, do the following:

1  From the Preset list, choose Edit Presets. The Edit Metadata Preset dialog box appears, which has the same entries as the Synchronize Metadata dialog box.

2  Fill in the metadata information you want to include in the preset and click Done.

3  In the Confirm dialog box, click Save As.

4  In the New Preset box, enter a descriptive name for the new preset.

5  Click Create.

If you apply a preset to a group of selected photos, Lightroom presents you with a dialog box (shown in Exhibit 2-23) asking if you want to apply the preset to the active photo or to all the selected photos.

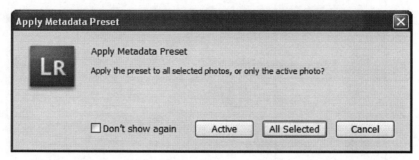

*Exhibit 2-23: The Apply Metadata Preset dialog box*

**Specify the active photo**

Earlier you learned that the first photo you select in a group selection is considered the active photo. If you want to make another photo in the selection the active photo, but you don't want to reselect the photos, click the photo you want to make active. If you click a selected photo, it becomes active without deselecting the other photos.

*Do it!*    **C-2:   Manipulating metadata**

| Here's how | Here's why |
|---|---|
| 1  In the Find panel, clear the **Text** check box | To view all the photos in the library again. |
| 2  In the Collections panel, select the **Natural beauty article** collection | |
| 3  Select the photo of a girl on a beach | |
| 4  In the right panel group, scroll down to view the Metadata panel | (If necessary.) A complete view of all the metadata included with the photos is shown, including the file name and camera data. It also shows that the photo is using the "My copyright" preset, which includes contact and copyright information you created when you imported some of the photos.<br><br>You'll view different metadata by choosing a different view. |
| 5  From the list in the title bar, choose **IPTC** | |
| | The panel changes to show the detailed contact and copyright information you created earlier. |
| 6  Select the sunset photo | This photo does not have the "My copyright" preset applied. You want to apply the copyright information to all the photos in this collection. |
| 7  Press ( CTRL ) + ( A ) | To select all six photos. |
| 8  In the Metadata panel, from the Preset list, choose **My copyright** | The Apply Metadata Preset dialog box appears. Even though one of the photos already has the preset applied, you can reapply it without any adverse results. This is quicker than selecting only the photos that don't have the preset. |
| Click **All Selected** | |
| 9  Press ( CTRL ) + ( D ) | To deselect the photos. You'll also add headline metadata to these photos. |

10 Select the sunset photo again

11 In the Metadata panel, in the
Content section, click in the box
to the right of Headline

The box becomes active.

In the box, type **Nightfall**

Press ( ↵ ENTER )                To add the metadata.

12 Add the following headlines to the       Select each photo and enter the headlines in the
remaining photos:                          Headline box in the Metadata panel.

Waterfall – Classic elegance
Girl – Beach fun
White dog – A pensive moment
Wet petals – After the rain
Blossoms – Springtime

13 Scroll to the bottom of the              To view the Copyright section. You realize that
Metadata panel                             you want to add information to the Rights Usage
                                           Terms field.

14 Press ( CTRL ) + ( A )                   To select all the photos.

In the Rights Usage Terms box,             To add the metadata.
type **No reproduction
without prior permission.**                You also want to add the rights usage metadata
and press ( ↵ ENTER )                       to the animal photos. You'll do this by
                                           synchronizing the animal photos with these.

15 In the Keyword Tags panel, click         To view all the photos with the "Animals"
**Animals**                                keyword applied.

16 Press ( CTRL ) + ( A )                   To select the photos.

17 In the Library panel, click              To view all the photos in the library. The animal
**All Photographs**                        photos are still selected.

18 Press ( CTRL ) and click the             To select one of the natural beauty article
blossoms photo                             photos. You want to synchronize the animal
                                           photos with this one, so you'll need to make the
                                           sunset photo the active photo.

Release ( CTRL ) and click the             To make it the active photo.
blossoms photo again

19 At the bottom of the right panel         To open the Synchronize Metadata dialog box.
group, click **Sync Metadata**

| | | |
|---|---|---|
| 20 | Clear **IPTC Content** | (If necessary.) To prevent the Headline metadata from being applied to the Natural beauty article photos. |
| 21 | Check **IPTC Copyright** | To synchronize the copyright metadata. |
| 22 | Check **IPTC Creator** | (If necessary.) To synchronize the creator metadata. |
| 23 | Click **Synchronize** | To update the metadata in the photos. |
| 24 | Click **Don't Save** | In the Confirm dialog box. |
| 25 | Press ( CTRL ) + ( D ) | To deselect the photos. |
| 26 | In the Keyword Tags panel, click **Animals** | To view all the photos with the "Animals" keyword applied. |
| | Select one of the photos | All the photos show the contact, copyright, and rights usage information. |
| 27 | View the entire library | In the Library panel, click All Photographs. |

# Topic D: Export options

*Explanation*

After you've made adjustments to photos, you might want to export them to another format. For example, you might want to e-mail photos to a client for their review, or you might need photos for a printed publication. You can export photos in PSD, JPG, TIFF, or DNG formats.

To export photos:

1 Using either the Grid or the Filmstrip, select the photos you want to export.

2 Do one of the following:

- At the bottom of the left panel group, click Export.
- Choose File, Export. Either method opens the Export dialog box, shown in Exhibit 2-24.

3 Do one of the following:

- If suitable, select a preset from the Preset list. Lightroom automatically configures the options based on the preset.
- If you want to set custom options, select the options you want in the dialog box. You can specify a folder to export to, adjust file naming and file type settings, set resolution and photo size options, and set a post-processing action, if necessary. To save the settings as a new preset, from the Preset list choose Save Current Settings as New Preset. A dialog box will allow you the name the new preset.

4 Click Export to export the photos.

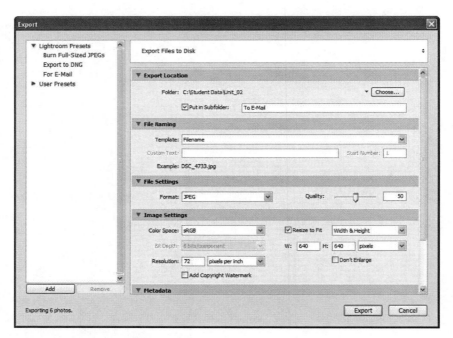

*Exhibit 2-24: The Export dialog box*

**Export presets**

The Presets list in the dialog box contains several presets, which are:

- **Burn Full-Sized JPEGs** – Exports photos as high-quality, full-sized JPEGs. Lightroom automatically sets the resolution to 240 ppi (which is suitable for printing), and exports the photos to a specific subfolder within the My Pictures folder on your computer. Also, a post-processing action is specified in the Post-processing section for burning the photos to a disc.

- **Export to DNG** – Exports photos to DNG format by using the photo's original file names. Also, no post-processing actions are specified.

- **For E-mail** – Exports photos to medium-quality JPEGs. Lightroom sets the resolution to 72 ppi (suitable for onscreen viewing). Also, a post-processing action is specified to show the photos in Windows Explorer.

**Post-processing actions**

The Post-processing actions section of the dialog box allows you to specify additional actions for the photos after they're exported. For example, you can specify that the photos be opened automatically in Photoshop, or even prepped for burning to a disc.

*Do it!*

**D-1: Exporting photos**

| Here's how | Here's why |
|---|---|
| 1 In the Collections panel, select **Natural beauty article** | To view the six photos you selected for the article. You'll export these photos in a format that you can e-mail to the client for them to review. |
| 2 Press ⌷CTRL⌷ + ⌷A⌷ | To select the photos. |
| 3 At the bottom of the left panel group, click **Export** | To open the Export dialog box. |
| 4 Expand the Lightroom Presets list | If necessary. |
| From the Preset list, select **For E-mail** | The options in the dialog box adjust for exporting photos appropriate for e-mail. You'll adjust the destination for the photos. |
| 5 To the right of Destination Folder, click **Choose** | The Browse For Folder dialog box appears. |
| Navigate to the current unit folder and click **OK** | |
| 6 Observe the settings in the dialog box | The settings reflect that the photos will be exported as JPEGs, have a resolution of 72 ppi, and a maximum width or height of 640 pixels. |
| 7 Observe the Post-processing setting | By default, the preset instructs Lightroom to show the photos in Windows Explorer after they are exported. You'll leave this setting as it is. |
| 8 Click **Export** | In the upper-left corner of the interface, in place of the identity plate, you can see the progress Lightroom makes as it exports the photos. When they're exported, a Windows Explorer window automatically opens and the photos are visible. |
| 9 Close the Windows Explorer window | To return to Lightroom. |

# Unit summary: The library

**Topic A**     In this topic, you learned how to **flag**, **rate**, **stack** and **sort** photos. You also **culled** photos by using Survey view.

**Topic B**     In this topic, you created and manipulated **keywords**. You also created specific **collections** of photos by using the Collections panel, and quickly assembled a temporary Quick Collection. Lastly, you **filtered** the photos visible in Grid view by entering criteria in the Find panel.

**Topic C**     In this topic, you synchronized **develop settings** within a group of selected photos. You also synchronized metadata adjustments.

**Topic D**     In this topic, you learned how to **export** photos in various formats by using the presets in the Export dialog box. You also learned about the **post-processing** actions you can choose.

## Independent practice activity

In this activity, you'll apply headings and keyword metadata to photos, organize photos into collections, and synchronize photos with the same settings.

1 In the Library, scroll down and select photos of the music rehearsal. Create a new collection titled **Band photos**. (*Hint:* With the photos selected, click the small plus sign on the right side of the Collections panel. Enter the title you want and click OK.)

2 Apply the My copyright preset to the photos. (*Hint:* With the photos selected, select My copyright from the Preset list in the Metadata panel.)

3 Apply the following metadata headlines to the photos in the collection: (*Hint:* Select each group of photos and enter the headlines in the Metadata panel.)
   - Photos 1 through 4: Sprocket band photos from 5/21 recording session.
   - Photo 5 and 6: Sprocket band photos from 6/10 concert in Chicago.

4 View the photos in the Lake folder (nested within the 2005-08-02 Lake folder).

5 Create a keyword named **Sunsets** and apply it to all of the photos. (*Hint:* Select all the photos; then click + on the right side of the Keyword Tags panel title bar.)

6 Within the same folder, apply the following ratings:
   - Photo 1: 2 stars
   - Photo 2: 4 stars
   - Photo 3: 5 stars
   - Photo 4: 4 stars
   - Photo 5: 4 stars
   - Photo 6: 3 stars
   - Photo 7: 5 stars
   - Photo 8: 2 stars

7 View the entire library, and filter the photos so that only those with three or more stars are visible. When you are finished, turn off the filter section in the Filmstrip to view all the photos in the Library again.

8 Stack the photos of the pink flowers. (*Hint:* To stack the selected photos, choose Photo, Stacking, Group into Stack.)

9  Add photos 52 through 55 to the Quick Collection. (*Hint:* To add the selected photos, press B.)

10  View the Quick Collection. (*Hint:* Click Quick Collection in the Library panel, or press Ctrl+B.)

11  Display all photos in the Library.

12  Select the first beach photo following the pink flower photos; then make some basic contrast and brightness adjustments to it using the Quick Develop panel.

13  Add the next photo to the selection; then synchronize the two photos with the settings applied to the first one. (*Hint:* Click Sync Settings at the bottom of the right panel group. Be sure to check Brightness and Contrast in the dialog box.)

14  View the Band photos collection and export the photos so that they can be e-mailed to the client for review. (*Hint:* In the Export dialog box, select the For E-mail preset. If necessary, set the destination folder to the current unit folder.)

## Review questions

1  Which are ways to rate photos? (Choose all that apply.)

A  Click the dots below a picture.

B  Double-click a photo and choose the number of stars you want.

C  Press 1 through 5 on the keyboard.

D  Ctrl-click a photo and choose the number of stars you want.

2  How can you remove a photo from Survey view? (Choose all that apply.)

A  Deselect the photo in the Filmstrip.

B  Double-click the photo.

C  Press Ctrl and click the photo.

D  Click the "x" in the lower-right corner of the photo.

3  How do you apply an existing keyword to other selected photos in the library?

A  Drag the keyword from the Keyword Tags panel to one of the photos.

B  Drag one of the photos to the keyword in the Keyword Tags panel.

C  Right-click one of the photos and choose the keyword you want to apply.

D  Double-click one of the photos, choose the keyword you want, and click OK.

4  How can you add a group of selected photos to the Quick Collection? (Choose all that apply.)

A  Click the small dot in the upper-right corner of one of the photos.

B  Press B.

C  Right-click one of the photos and choose Add To Quick Collection.

D  Drag one of the photos to Quick Collection in the Library panel.

# Unit 3

## Developing photos

**Unit time: 120 minutes**

Complete this unit, and you'll know how to:

**A** Apply presets to photos, adjust white balance, and make basic tonal adjustments.

**B** Use history steps to revert to previous versions of photos, create snapshots, and compare before and after versions of photos.

**C** Adjust tone curves, make precise shadow and highlight adjustments, and adjust color.

**D** Convert photos to grayscale and create split-tone effects.

**E** Crop and straighten photos.

**F** Make precise detail adjustments.

**G** Copy and paste adjustments between photos, and create custom presets.

# Topic A: Basic adjustments

*Explanation*

You can use Lightroom to adjust colors and contrast to correct photo problems, enhance realism, or achieve other goals. Keep in mind any adjustments you make to photos in Lightroom are non-destructive.

## Basic photo adjustment principles

Although photo adjustments are somewhat subjective, there are some basic principles that most people agree on.

- **Maximize contrast and saturation** – Most people agree that a high-contrast photo is more interesting and engaging than a low-contrast photo. You should generally increase contrast as much as possible while maintaining a realistic photo.

- **Avoid clipping highlights and shadows** – As you increase contrast, try to avoid clipping highlights or shadows. *Clipping* occurs when increasing or decreasing the contrast converts multiple brightness levels to a single shade. When this occurs, you lose photo detail that you can't get back. For example, if you increase contrast too much, a white sidewalk with many subtle color variations in it might become completely white, destroying all sense of texture and realism. To avoid clipping highlights and shadows, it's often best to set the brightest areas slightly darker than pure white, and set the darkest areas to slightly brighter than pure black.

- **Adjust photos based on what looks good** – As you adjust a photo, you don't need to focus on trying to perfectly capture the contrast and saturation of the original scene. Instead, adjust the photo to make it appear the way you want. You'll often end up with a photo that has more contrast and saturation than the original photo. For some photos, you might want to retain low contrast for realism, or you might even want to lower the contrast for artistic reasons. However, people generally respond better to photos that "pop" with contrast and saturation.

## The Presets panels

Some photos might benefit from one of the preset adjustments included within the Presets panel, shown in Exhibit 3-1. The panel includes several basic tone curve adjustments as well as presets to convert images to grayscale or duotones. You can preview the presets by pointing to them and observing the effects in the Navigator panel. To apply a preset, click it.

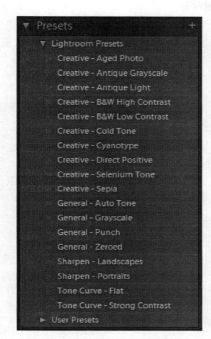

*Exhibit 3-1: The Presets panel*

*Do it!*

## A-1: Applying presets

| Here's how | Here's why |
|---|---|
| 1 In the Library panel, click **All Photographs** | (If necessary.) To view the library. |
| 2 Select the washed-out photo of two zebras | |
| | The photo should be 25 in the index. |
| 3 Switch to the Develop module | Click Develop in the upper-right corner of the interface, or press Ctrl+Alt+2. |
| 4 In the left panel group, expand the Navigator panel | If necessary. |
| 5 In the Presets panel, point to each of the presets | The Navigator panel displays the effect of the preset. You want to increase the contrast while retaining color. |
| 6 Click **Tone Curve – Strong Contrast** | The preset increases the contrast in the photo somewhat. |

## White balance

*Explanation*

Digital photos often appear with a *color cast*, which is a color that appears subtly throughout the photo and that might be particularly noticeable in areas that should be neutral. *White balance* is the process of removing unrealistic color casts, so that objects that appear white in person are rendered white in your photo.

Earlier you learned about the benefits of working with camera RAW files, including the ability to more accurately adjust the white balance. If you set a camera to Daylight white balance, but shoot pictures inside, they'll tend to look orange because tungsten lights are more red-orange than daylight. With a JPEG image, you can still adjust the white balance after the fact, but it can be hard to completely fix, as the Red color channel may have blown out some of the information. In contrast, RAW files don't have a white balance locked in. So, if you set the wrong white balance on the camera, you can select a new white balance preset in Lightroom. To adjust the white balance with a preset, select one from the WB (White Balance) list in the Basic panel, shown in Exhibit 3-2. When you select a preset, the Temp and Tint slider values are adjusted automatically.

White Balance Selector tool

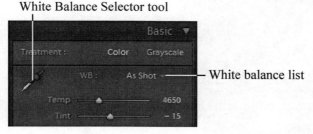

White balance list

*Exhibit 3-2: White balance options in the Basic panel*

You can also more precisely set white balance by specifying a pixel to sample from. Many photos have some areas that are neutral (areas without a color tint). You can use one of these neutral areas, even a dark gray one, to help fine-tune the white balance. To do this, click the White Balance Selector tool in the upper-left corner of the panel, then point to a neutral area of the photo. When you point to the photo, a magnified view of the pixels in the area appear within a pop-up grid, and the RGB values for the pixel are displayed at the bottom, as shown in Exhibit 3-3. The center box represents the pixel you're sampling. RGB values for neutral areas should approximately match. For example, a neutral middle gray would have R, G, and B values all very close to 50%. To adjust the white balance, click the White Balance Selector tool on the pixel you've selected.

When you position the White Balance Selector tool on a photo, the surrounding pixels are visible in a grid.

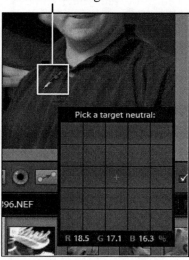

*Exhibit 3-3: Adjusting white balance by using the White Balance Selector tool*

If you've selected the White Balance Selector tool, but decide not to adjust the white balance, press Esc or click again in the upper-left corner of the Basic panel to deselect the tool.

### Resetting photos

You can quickly remove adjustments from photos by clicking the Reset button at the bottom of the right panel group. Doing so removes all adjustments, even adjustments you applied as you imported them.

*Do it!*    **A-2:    Adjusting white balance**

| Here's how | Here's why |
| --- | --- |
| 1  Using the Filmstrip, select photo **DSC_3896**, as shown |  |
| | (The grayscale picture of a man.) The photo was converted to grayscale when you imported it, but you now want to work with the original color version. |
| 2  At the bottom of the right panel group, click **Reset** | To remove the grayscale adjustment and return the photo to its original colors. |
| | This picture has reasonable lighting, but poor white balance, giving it a red cast. You'll adjust the white balance. |
| 3  In the right panel group, in the Basic panel, from the WB list, select several of the options to see their effect | 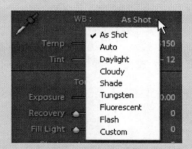 |
| | The Flash and Daylight presets are closest to being correct, because this photo was taken with a flash bounced off the ceiling. |
| 4  Select the **Flash** preset and observe the Temperature value | The temperature of 5500 approximates that of a camera flash, but doesn't account for factors such as ambient light and the color of the ceiling the flash was bounced off. |
| | You'll fine-tune the white balance by targeting an area that should be neutral in color. The man is wearing a black shirt, so you can use a gray area of the shirt for reference. |
| 5  In the upper-left corner of the panel, click the White Balance Selector tool |  |
| | To select it. |

| | | |
|---|---|---|
| 6 | Point the tip of the tool on a lighter gray area on the man's shirt, and observe the R, G, and B values |  |

When you point to a gray area in the shirt, a magnified view of the pixels in that area appear.

The R (Red) value is a bit higher than the G (Green), which is a bit higher than B (Blue) one, indicating that the photo has a slight reddish cast.

| | | |
|---|---|---|
| 7 | Click the gray area on the man's shirt | Lightroom neutralizes that color by adjusting the Temp and Tint slider values. The Temperature is now lower than it was (probably between 4600 and 5100K), removing the red cast, and the Tint is a negative color, helping to balance out the R, G, and B values. |
| 8 | Select the White Balance Selector tool, then point to the same area again | Now the RGB values are very similar. |
| 9 | Press ( ESC ) | To deselect the White Balance Selector tool. |

## Tonal range

*Explanation*

*Tonal range* refers to the maximum range of tones visible in a photo. The lightest part of a photo is called the *highlight* and the darkest is called the *shadow*. Ideally, a photo with the widest possible tonal range will have some pixels that are pure white (highlight) and some that are pure black (shadow), providing the fullest possible contrast. However, for a variety of reasons, such as photographer error or even low-contrast subject matter, most photos fall short of that. The tonal range of a photo is the numeric difference between the photo's maximum highlight pixel and its minimum shadow pixel.

**The Histogram panel**

The Histogram panel provides a graphical representation of the tonal range of a photo. The preview consists of overlaying RGB channels. Each channel shows a range of tones. Because most photos have a fairly continuous range, the channels blend together to form a "mountainous" appearance, as shown in Exhibit 3-4. The left side of the histogram represents darker pixels, the right side represents brighter pixels, and the center represents midtone pixels. For example, if the histogram appears very tall at the left side, this indicates that the photo has many dark pixels.

If a photo's histogram does not extend all the way to the left or right in the panel, the photo does not contain a full tonal range and usually has weak contrast. You can adjust the tonal range by using the Exposure, Recovery, Fill Light, and Blacks sliders in the Basic panel. Alternately, you can make adjustments by dragging within the histogram itself. Depending on where you point in the histogram, it triggers one of the four sliders to become active, as shown in Exhibit 3-4. If you drag in the histogram, the corresponding slider will move in the direction you are dragging.

One approach to color-correcting photos with a weak tonal range is to move the Exposure and Blacks sliders until the histogram spans the width of the panel. This forces the photo's darkest pixels to black, and lightest pixels to white. Although this method of maximizing contrast often yields good results, it's not a failsafe formula, because not all photos should display the full range of tones from black to white.

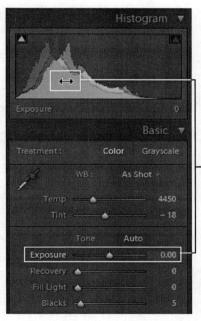

Pointing to an area in the Histogram panel activates one of the four tonal sliders in the Basic panel.

*Exhibit 3-4: Adjusting tonal range by using the Histogram panel*

*Do it!*

## A-3: Adjusting tonal range

| Here's how | Here's why |
|---|---|
| 1 Use the Filmstrip to select the faded photo of the zebras again | 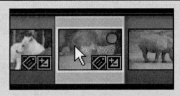<br><br>Photo DSC_1438. |
| 2 In the Histogram panel, observe the photo's histogram | 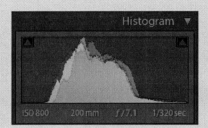<br><br>This photo is very weak in overall contrast because the lightest areas (on the right side of the "mountain" shape) are far from pure white, and the darkest areas (on the left) are far from pure black.<br><br>You'll increase the exposure to make the photo's lightest areas nearly white. |
| 3 In the Histogram panel, point as shown | 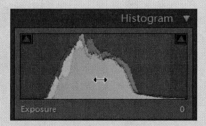<br><br>When you point to the center of the histogram, the Exposure slider in the Basic panel looks brighter, indicating it is active. |
| 4 Move the pointer to the left and right on the histogram | (Be sure to just move the pointer. Do not drag in the histogram.) As you move the pointer, each one of the four tonal sliders in the Basic panel is activated. |

5  Position the pointer so that the Exposure slider is active, and then slowly drag to the right

To begin increasing the Exposure value. As you drag, the histogram begins to shift to the right. Also, the Exposure slider in the Basic panel begins moving to the right.

When the right edge of the histogram nearly reaches the right side of the panel (at approximately +0.82), stop dragging

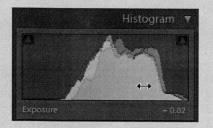

This adjustment brightened the photo appreciably. Stopping short of the right edge prevented highlight areas from getting blown out (where pure white areas with no detail appear).

The photo still needs the tonal range expanded to darken the dark areas.

6  Point near the left edge of the histogram so that the Blacks slider is active in the Basic panel

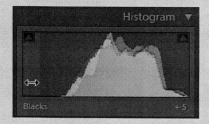

Slowly drag to the left until the left edge of the histogram nearly reaches the left side of the panel (at approximately +52)

The photo contrast is improved dramatically from the original. It could still use tonal adjustment to bring out detail, particularly in the dark areas on the right, but the overall range of tones is appropriate for the subject matter.

## Midtones

*Explanation*

After you've set the overall tonal scale by using the Exposure, Recovery, Fill Light, and Blacks sliders, you can fine-tune brightness and contrast by using the midtone sliders, shown in Exhibit 3-5. The Brightness and Contrast sliders do not affect the tonal range as sharply. For example, if you drag the Brightness slider all the way to the right, the photo will look extremely washed out and difficult to see, but none of the pixels will be clipped to pure white.

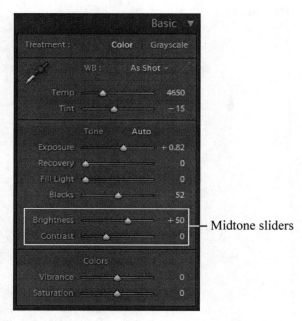

*Exhibit 3-5: Midtone sliders in the Basic panel*

*Do it!*

## A-4:    Adjusting midtones

| Here's how | Here's why |
|---|---|
| 1  In the Basic panel, scroll down to view the Brightness and Contrast sliders | (If necessary.) While initially increasing contrast via the preset helped the photo, the combination of that added contrast and the expansion of the tonal range pushed many dark gray pixels to nearly black.<br><br>Lowering the contrast helps bring back details that were lost, particularly in the dark areas. |
| 2  Drag the Contrast slider to a value of approximately –36 | Brightness ——————— + 50<br>Contrast ——————— – 36<br><br>This lightens the midtones, opening up a bit more detail in the rocks behind the zebras. |
| 3  Drag the Brightness slider to a value of approximately +26 | |

# Topic B:  Managing adjustments

*Explanation*

After you start making adjustments to a photo, you might want to revert back to a prior state, or you might want to compare an adjustment you've made with the way the photo looked before. You can use the History and Snapshots panels and Before and After views to help manage adjustments.

## The History panel

If you make multiple adjustments to a photo, and then decide you want to jump back several steps, or even revert back to the way it was when you imported it, you can do so using the History panel, shown in Exhibit 3-6. The History panel shows a list of adjustments applied to a photo. By default, the first entry will be the state of the photo when you first imported it. Each time you make an adjustment, it is recorded as an additional step in the list. To revert back to a prior version, click one of the preceding steps. You can also clear the steps in the History panel by clicking Clear on the right side of the panel title bar.

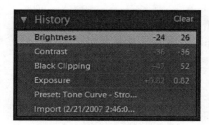

*Exhibit 3-6: The History panel*

## The Snapshots panel

If you've made a lot of adjustments, the number of steps in the History panel can become confusing. To manage adjustments, you can create snapshots of a photo by using the Snapshots panel, shown in Exhibit 3-7. To create a snapshot, click the plus sign on the right side of the panel title bar. When you do, a new snapshot appears in the panel. Enter a descriptive name for the snapshot and press Enter. You can also create snapshots by right-clicking a step in the History panel and choosing Create Snapshot.

*Exhibit 3-7: The Snapshots panel*

*Do it!*

## B-1:  Working with the History and Snapshots panels

| Here's how | Here's why |
|---|---|
| 1  In the left panel group, observe the History panel | The panel shows a list of steps you've performed on the selected photo. |
| 2  Click **Preset: Tone Curve - Strong** | |
| | (To return the photo to the state just after applying that adjustment.) |
| | The photo appears washed out again. |
| 3  Click **Brightness -24 26** | (To reapply the most recent adjustments.) |
| | You'll create a snapshot of the photo in this state, so you can easily return to it later, if necessary. |
| 4  Right-click Brightness -24 26 and choose **Create Snapshot** | |
| | A new snapshot appears in the Snapshot panel. |
| Type **Basic range and contrast adjustments** and press ⏎ ENTER | To rename the snapshot. |

## Before and After views

*Explanation*

If the adjustments you make to photos are subtle, it might be difficult to tell whether you're really improving them. To help with this, you can compare before and after versions of a photo for each adjustment you make. To do this, click the Before and After Views button in the toolbar (as shown in Exhibit 3-8), or select one of the four Before and After settings from the button drop-down list. The Before version shows the photo prior to the last adjustment you made; not the photo as you originally imported it. If the photo is magnified, you can shift the visible area by dragging in either window.

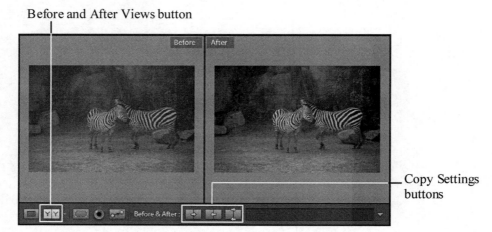

*Exhibit 3-8: Before and After options*

The following table shows each of the four Before/After settings you can select from the button drop-down list.

| Button | Description | Example |
|---|---|---|
| Before/After Left/Right | (Default) Shows the before and after versions of the photo side-by-side. If the photo is magnified, the visible areas are the same in both versions. | |
| Before/After Left/Right Split | Shows the before and after versions of the photo by vertically splitting it in half. In order to use a split view, the photo magnification must be Fill, 1:1, or 3:1. | |
| Before/After Top/Bottom | Shows the before and after versions of the photo above and below. If the photo is magnified, the visible areas are the same. | |
| Before/After Top/Bottom Split | Shows the before and after versions of the photo by horizontally splitting it in half. In order to use a split view, the photo magnification must be Fill, 1:1, or 3:1. | |

**Updating before and after versions**

You might want to update the Before and After views as you work. For example, you might decide to keep an adjustment, and want to update the Before version to reflect the change before you make another adjustment. To update either view, you can click the Copy Settings buttons in the toolbar, shown in Exhibit 3-8. You can also swap the before and after settings by using the third button.

*Do it!*

## B-2: Comparing before and after versions of photos

| Here's how | Here's why |
|---|---|
| 1 In the toolbar, click [Y│Y] | To display Before and After views of the photo. |
| 2 Click either version of the photo | To zoom both Before and After views to 1:1 magnification. |
| Drag either of the photos left and right | Both views scroll to display the same area. |
| | The After version is much better than the Before version, but you still think the photo has room for improvement. You'll set the current After view to the Before view, so you can compare future changes you make to what you've done so far. |
| 3 In the toolbar, click [⇦] | To set the Before view to match the After one. |
| 4 Click either version of the photo | To return to Fit magnification. The versions match. You'll compare a further edited version of the photo to this one after you apply more adjustments. |

# Topic C:   Tone curves and color adjustments

*Explanation*

You can make more precise tonal adjustments to photos by using tone curves. You can also enhance photo colors by using the HSL and Color panels.

### Tone curve graphs

To make tone curve adjustments, you use the Tone Curve panel, located in the right panel group. The panel shows a tone curve graph as well as Highlight, Shadow, and Midtone tonal sliders. You can use the tone curve graph to make more precise changes to the tonal scale of a photo. The background of the graph shows a simplified version of the selected photo's histogram, as shown in Exhibit 3-9.

The horizontal axis in the graph represents the original tone values, or input values. The lower-left corner represents the darkest (black) values and progresses to the right for lighter (white) values. The vertical axis represents changed tone values, or output values. The lower-left corner designates the darkest values and progresses toward the top for lighter values.

Running diagonally across the graph is a 45° line you use to make the adjustments. If a photo has no tonal adjustments applied to it, the line will be straight. You make tonal adjustments by shifting a portion of the line up or down, creating "curves" in the line. Curving the line upward lightens tones and curving the line downward darkens them.

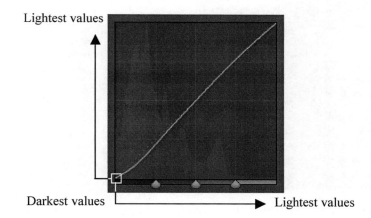

*Exhibit 3-9: An example of a tone curve graph*

## Tone curve adjustments

To make tone curve adjustments, do one of the following:

- Point to an area on the graph and drag up or down to make the adjustment. When you point to the graph, a dot appears on the line indicating the tonal area being adjusted, as shown in the example in Exhibit 3-10. Also, similar to the Histogram panel, the horizontal position of the pointer on the graph triggers the corresponding sliders below the graph. In the example below, the horizontal position of the pointer is triggering the Darks slider.

- Click the Adjust Tone Curve by Dragging button in the upper-left corner of the panel; then drag directly on the photo to adjust the curve. When you point to a specific area in the photo, a dot appears on the curve indicating the lightness value of the pixel you're pointing to.

- Drag the Highlights, Lights, Darks, or Shadows sliders beneath the curve.

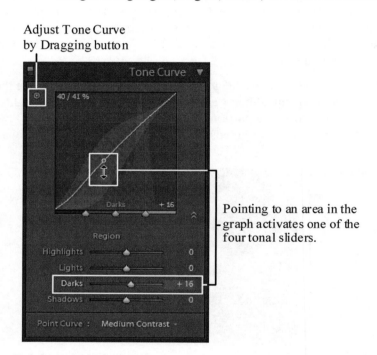

Adjust Tone Curve
by Dragging button

Pointing to an area in the
graph activates one of the
four tonal sliders.

*Exhibit 3-10: The Tone Curve panel*

*Do it!*

## C-1:   Adjusting tones by using a tone curve

| Here's how | Here's why |
|---|---|
| 1  Press Ⓓ | To switch to Loupe view. |
| 2  Use the Filmstrip to select the photo of tree blossoms | <br><br>Photo DSC_2918. |
| 3  In the right panel group, scroll down to view the Tone Curve panel | (If necessary.) Depending on the size of your monitor, the lower part of the panel might be hidden. You'll hide the Filmstrip so you can see the panel more clearly. |
| 4  Click the small triangle at the bottom of the interface | <br><br>To hide the Filmstrip. |
| 5  In the panel, point to the left side of the curve, as shown | 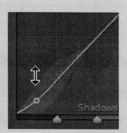<br><br>A dot appears on the lower-left part of the curve and the Shadows slider becomes active. |
|    Slowly move the pointer from left to right | As you move across the curve the dot moves up, and the midtone and highlight sliders become active. |

| | |
|---|---|
| 6 Point to the lower-left side of the curve again, as shown |  |
| | The Shadows slider should be active. |
| Slowly drag down | To begin to darken the shadow tones in the photo. As you drag, the Shadows slider begins to move to the left. |
| Drag down until the Shadows slider is approximately –34 | The darker shadow tones give the photo more contrast. |
| | You'll continue to make tonal adjustments by dragging directly within the photo. |
| 7 In the upper-left corner of the panel, click the Adjust Tone Curve button |  |
| 8 Point anywhere on the photo | As you move the pointer over the photo, the curve shows the tonal area correlating to the brightness of the pixels you're pointing to. |
| 9 Point to a white area in one of the flower petals, as shown |  |
| | The highlights portion of the curve becomes active, as well as the Highlights slider. |
| Slowly drag up | To begin lightening the highlight tones in the photo. As you drag, the Highlights slider begins to move to the right. |
| Drag up until the Highlights slider is approximately +31 | You want to brighten the white midtones in the sky in the background. |

10  Point to the sky near the left side of the photo

The Lights slider in the panel becomes active.

Slowly drag up until the Lights slider is approximately +15

You'll create a snapshot of the photo so that you can compare it to the original version.

11  Press (ESC)

To deselect the Adjust Tone Curve button.

12  In the History panel, right-click the most recent step and choose **Create Snapshot**

A new snapshot appears in the Snapshots panel.

Title the snapshot **Highlights 31, Lights 15, Shadows -34**

To describe all the adjustments you've done so far.

13  In the Snapshot panel, click **Import**

To revert the photo to the way it was originally.

14  Click **Highlights 31, Lights 15, Shadows -34**

The one you adjusted has better contrast and more vibrant color.

## Shadows

*Explanation*

The most prominent tonal changes in photos occur when you make highlight or shadow adjustments. You can use them to bring out hidden details in photos and make more precise contrast improvements. In this section, you'll learn how to fine-tune shadow adjustments.

### Region sliders

By default, the tone curve graph is divided horizontally into four sections. Each section correlates to one of the tonal sliders, as shown in Exhibit 3-11. This provides an evenly spaced range for each of the tonal areas. You can make more precise tonal adjustments by making certain ranges wider or narrower. To do this, drag the Region sliders located just below the graph to the left or right.

For example, if you were to drag the left-most region slider to the right, any adjustments you make using the Shadows slider would affect a broader range of tones in the photo. Also, any adjustments you make using the Darks slider would affect a smaller tonal range.

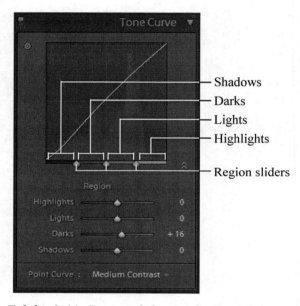

*Exhibit 3-11: Region sliders in the Tone Curve panel*

*Do it!*

## C-2: Adjusting shadows

| Here's how | Here's why |
|---|---|
| 1  Use the Filmstrip to select photo DSC_4736 |  |
| | You'll have to temporarily view the Filmstrip by pointing to the triangle at the bottom of the interface. |
| 2  In the Basic panel, drag the Contrast slider to a value of +74 | As with the tree blossoms photo, the dark parts of the photo become darker. The sky color is richer, but the rocks in the foreground are now nearly completely silhouetted. You'll use the tone curve to brighten the rocks. |
| 3  In the Tone Curve panel, drag the Shadows slider to a value of approximately +78 | This adjustment makes the rocks visible. However, it also brightened the water significantly. |
| 4  In the History panel, alternately click the last two steps | To clearly see the tonal change in the photo. |
| In the History panel, click **Shadow Tones** | (If necessary.) So the photo shows the tonal adjustment. You'll adjust the left-most region slider to narrow the range of tones the Shadows slider affects. |
| 5  Beneath the tone curve, drag the left-most region slider to the left | 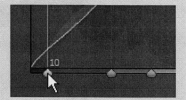 |
| | Until it won't go any further. |
| 6  In the History panel, alternately click the last two steps | To clearly see the change in the photo. |
| In the History panel, click **Shadow Split** | To switch back to the current version again. The region slider targeted a much narrower gamut of dark pixels in the photo, thus the rocks are lighter, but the water remains darker. |
| 7  Save a snapshot named **Adjusted contrast and shadows** | |

## Highlights

*Explanation*

You can fine-tune highlight adjustments to bring out detail in light areas of photos.

### Highlight and shadow clipping

It can be hard to adjust clipped areas of photos. In a clipped area, the pixel tones are so dark or so light that they are pure black or white. You'll usually want to avoid this in photos as much as possible. To help identify clipped areas, you can use the clipping indicators in the upper corners of the Histogram, as shown in Exhibit 3-12. The left indicator shows pure black pixels, and the right indicator shows pure white.

To view clipped areas, point to or click one of the indicators. When you do, the clipped areas in the photo are colored as blue (for black pixels) or red (for white pixels). If you click an indicator, the clipped area preview remains visible so that you can make adjustments to remove it.

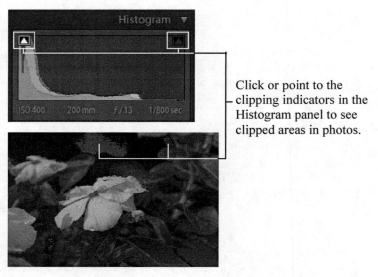

Click or point to the clipping indicators in the Histogram panel to see clipped areas in photos.

*Exhibit 3-12: An example of previewing a clipped area in a photo*

*Do it!*    **C-3:   Adjusting highlights**

| Here's how | Here's why |
|---|---|
| 1  Use the Filmstrip to select photo DSC_0582 |  |
| | (You'll have to temporarily view the Filmstrip by pointing to the triangle at the bottom of the interface.) |
| | You'll brighten this flower and the leaves behind it without sacrificing fine highlight detail. |
| 2  In the Histogram panel, observe the histogram | The histogram is very tall at the left edge, indicating that there's probably very little detail in the darkest parts of the photo. You'll verify this with the Shadow clipping indicator. |
| 3  In the top-left corner of the Histogram panel, point to the Shadow clipping indicator | 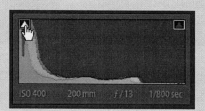 |
| | When you point to the indicator, certain areas of the photo look blue, indicating areas where clipping is occurring (areas that are pure black). |
|     Click the clipping indicator | To keep it turned on. |
| 4  In the Basic panel, drag the Blacks slider to the left to a value of 0 | Almost all the blue clipped areas in the photo disappear. |
| 5  In the Histogram panel, click the Shadows clipping indicator | To turn off shadow clipping preview. |
| 6  Observe the right side of the histogram | The photo's brightest areas are far from the right edge, indicating that you could brighten it overall without losing highlight detail. However, you could also easily clip some highlight areas, so you'll turn on the highlight warning. |

7  In the Histogram panel, click the Highlight clipping indicator

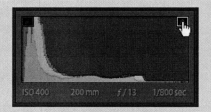

Currently, there are no highlight areas that are clipped, so no highlighting is visible in the photo.

8  Drag the Exposure slider to a value of approximately +2.12

The photo brightens appreciably, but some red highlights appear on the white flower, indicating that some clipping is occurring.

9  Drag the Exposure slider to a value of approximately +1.65

A few very small areas of red remain. Because the clipping is very small, you'll leave it.

10  In the Histogram panel, click the Highlight clipping indicator

To turn it off.

11  Create a snapshot named **Basic adjustments only**

While the flower's highlights aren't clipped much, there isn't much visible detail in some areas near the center. You'll darken the highlights overall.

12  Click the center of the flower's front petal, as shown

To magnify the photo to 1:1.

13  Scroll down to view the sliders in the Tone Curve panel

14  Drag the Highlights slider to a value of −72

(To even out the tone in the flower and return more detail to some light areas.) Some water droplets appear in areas that formerly appeared nearly pure white.

15  Under the tone curve, drag the rightmost region slider to the left to approximately 62

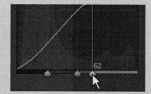

To expand the tonal range, further accentuating the water droplets and brightening the very brightest areas.

16  Drag the photo to the right as necessary to view the left petal

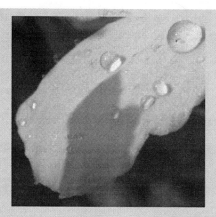

(The petal has a shadow cast upon its tip)

You'll control the brightness of this shadow by moving the middle region slider.

17  Drag the middle region slider to the left to approximately 30

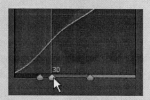

Narrowing the Darks region darkened the shadow, making it more prominent.

18  Click the photo

To zoom back out to Fit magnification.

19  Create a snapshot named **All adjustments**

20  Compare the Import, Basic adjustments only, and All adjustments snapshots

The original was too dark overall; the Basic adjustments only version had excessively bright contrast, but the All adjustments version brightens the background without clipping the highlights.

21  Click **All adjustments**

To keep the adjustments you made.

## Color adjustments

*Explanation*

In addition to tonal adjustments, you might also want to adjust color hues or increase or decrease color saturation in photos. You can make color adjustments by using the HSL and Color panels in the HSL/Color/Grayscale color panel group, shown in Exhibit 3-13. The two panels produce similar results, but they organize the sliders in different ways.

The HSL panel shows four color categories at the top: Hue, Saturation, Luminance, and All. The color sliders in each category are identical, but they produce different results. For example, if you wanted to make red colors in a photo brighter, you could select the Luminance category and make the adjustment by using the Red slider.

The Color panel shows Hue, Saturation, and Luminance sliders, and has a row of color chips along the top. To make a color adjustment by using this panel, select the color chip you want and drag one (or more) of the sliders.

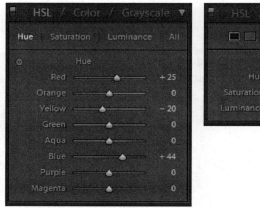

*Exhibit 3-13: HSL and Color options in the HSL/Color/Grayscale panel*

### Global color adjustments

You can also make global color adjustments by using the Colors section of the Basics panel. The panel includes two sliders: Vibrance and Saturation. When you make adjustments by using either of these sliders, all the colors in the photo are affected.

*Do it!*

## C-4: Adjusting specific colors

| Here's how | Here's why |
|---|---|
| 1 Using the Filmstrip, select photo DSC_4733 | 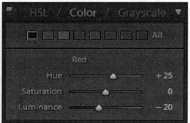 |
| | (You'll have to temporarily view the Filmstrip by pointing to the triangle at the bottom of the interface.) |
| | You'll make the yellows in the sky more saturated, but you'll also make them more orange in hue. |

| | | |
|---|---|---|
| 2 | In the right panel group, scroll down to view the HSL/Color/Grayscale panel | By default, the HSL panel is active. |
| 3 | In the panel, drag the Yellows slider to the left to approximately –40 | The yellow areas of the sky become more orange. |
| 4 | At the top of the panel, click **Saturation** | To switch to the saturation sliders. |
| | Drag the Yellow slider to approximately +50 | To make the more yellow-orange areas of the sky a bit more vivid. |
| 5 | At the top of the panel, click **Luminance** | To switch to the Luminance sliders. |
| | Drag the Yellow slider to approximately –20 | To further deepen the sky.<br><br>Lastly, you'll shift the color of the blue clouds slightly toward purple. This time, you'll use the Color panel. |
| 6 | In the panel title bar, click **Color** | To switch to the Color panel. |
| 7 | In the panel, click the blue color chip | To make it active. |
| 8 | Drag the Hue slider to approximately +85 | To make the darker clouds more of a purple color. |
| 9 | Create a snapshot named **Color adjustments** | |
| 10 | Compare the Import and Color adjustments snapshots | The new version is more vibrant than the original. |
| 11 | Click **Color adjustments** | To keep the adjustments you made. |

# Topic D:  Grayscale and split toning

*Explanation*

Other adjustments you might want to apply to photos include converting them to grayscale and perhaps applying split tone effects.

## Grayscale conversion

There are multiple ways to convert a photo to grayscale. Within the Develop module, you can:

- Click Grayscale Conversion in the Presets panel. This method also applies several default contrast and tonal adjustments.
- Click Grayscale in the Treatment section in the Basic panel.
- Click Grayscale in the HSL/Color/Grayscale panel title bar.
- Choose Develop, Convert to Grayscale.
- Press the keyboard shortcut V. (This also works in the Library module.)

After you've converted a photo to grayscale, you can make further contrast and tonal adjustments by using either the Basic or Grayscale panels. The Grayscale panel is included in the HSL/Color/Grayscale panel group, as shown in Exhibit 3-14.

*Exhibit 3-14: Grayscale options in the HSL/Color/Grayscale panel*

*Do it!*

## D-1: Converting a photo to grayscale

| Here's how | Here's why |
|---|---|
| 1  Use the Filmstrip to select photo DSC_3199 | |
| | You'll convert this photo to grayscale and optimize its contrast and tonality. You'll start by using the grayscale preset. |
| 2  In the left panel group, in the Presets panel, click **General - Grayscale** | To convert the photo to grayscale using Lightroom's default settings. |
| 3  Create a snapshot named **Default grayscale** | You'll increase the exposure of the photo slightly to increase its overall contrast. |
| 4  In the right panel group, in the Basic panel, drag the Exposure slider to a value of approximately +0.23 | |
| Drag the Blacks slider to a value of approximately 35 | To darken the shadow areas. |
| 5  Scroll down to view the HSL/Color/Grayscale panel | When you converted the photo to grayscale using the preset, Lightroom automatically activated the Grayscale panel. |
| | You'll adjust some color values, but you'll first examine the color version of the photo to see which colors are prominent. |
| 6  In the panel title bar, click **Color** | |
| | To switch back to a color version of the photo. This picture has a lot of red in the brick tower, as well as blue inside the windows at the top. |
| In the panel title bar, click **Grayscale** | To display the photo in grayscale again. |

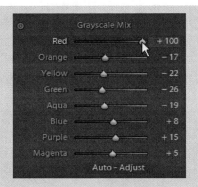

7  Drag the Red slider to the maximum value of 100

To emphasize red areas in the grayscale conversion. The brick areas brighten a bit, and the lettering on the tower becomes more legible because the background behind it lightens.

Drag the Blue slider to a value of −22

To darken the area within the tower's windows at the top.

8  Create a snapshot named **Adjusted grayscale**

Compare the Adjusted grayscale and Default grayscale snapshots

The adjusted version is much brighter and contains more contrast and detail than the default conversion.

9  Click **Adjusted grayscale**

To keep the adjusted version.

# Split toning

You can add color to grayscale photos by using presets in the Presets panel or options in the Split Toning panel. In the Presets panel, you can apply the Sepia Tone or Cyanotype presets, which make grayscale photos look more brown or blue. The sepia effect (brown) is commonly used to make photos look older.

You can also apply color using the Split Toning panel, shown in Exhibit 3-15. You can apply a single color throughout the tonal range, or you can apply two colors; one color for shadows and one for highlights.

If you apply a single color, you can use the Hue and Saturation sliders in the Highlights section to create the color you want. Hue sets the color of the tone. Saturation sets the strength of the color.

If you apply two colors, you can use the Hue and Saturation sliders in the Shadows section for the second color. The Balance slider sets the strength of either the Highlights or Shadows. Positive values increase the strength of the Shadows sliders, and negative values increase the strength of the Highlights sliders.

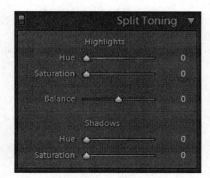

*Exhibit 3-15: The Split Toning panel*

**Preview colors**

By default, grayscale photos have default Highlight and Shadow saturation settings of 0, which is why they look black and white. If you drag the Hue sliders without changing the saturation setting, the color change won't be apparent in the photo. However, if you press Alt as you drag the sliders, you can preview and select the color you want before adjusting the saturation.

*Do it!*

## D-2: Split-toning a photo

| Here's how | Here's why |
|---|---|
| 1 Use the Filmstrip to select photo DSC_4330 | |
| 2 In the HSL/Color/Grayscale panel title bar, click **Grayscale** | To convert the photo to grayscale. |
| 3 Scroll down to view the Split Toning panel | You'll apply two colors to the grayscale, making the highlights (largely the rocks) a green tint, and the shadow areas (largely the water) a blue tint. |
| 4 Under Highlights, drag the Hue slider to the right and observe the effect | The Hue slider has no effect until you increase the saturation. However, you can preview the effect of the color by pressing Alt. |
| Hold down (ALT) as you drag the Hue slider | The hue tints the photo highlights as if it were applied at 100% saturation. |
| Set the hue at approximately 85 and release (ALT) | |
| 5 Drag the Saturation slider to approximately 50 | To tint the highlight areas with green. |
| 6 Under Shadows, hold down (ALT) as you drag the Hue slider | To preview the effect of tinting the shadows with a color. The color you chose will predominantly tint the water. |
| Set the hue at approximately 235 and release (ALT) | |
| 7 Drag the Saturation slider to approximately 60 | To tint the shadow areas with blue. You'll also experiment with sepia toning, which is a form of split toning. |
| 8 Use the Filmstrip to select photo DSC_3199 | |
| | (The grayscale clock tower.) You'll preview the sepia preset in the Presets panel. |
| 9 In the Presets panel, click **Creative - Sepia** | |

| | |
|---|---|
| 10  Examine the Split Toning panel | This preset tints the photo with the same brown color for both highlights and shadows. You'll reduce the saturation in the shadows to make the effect subtler. |
| 11  In the panel, under Shadows, set the Saturation to approximately 21 | To allow black areas to show through without being significantly tinted. |
| 12  Create a snapshot named **Subtle sepia** | |

# Topic E:  Cropping and straightening

*Explanation*

You might need to crop and/or straighten photos. Keep in mind that all adjustments in Lightroom are non-destructive, and this includes cropping and straightening. After you crop or straighten a photo, you can revert back to its original dimensions at any time.

## Cropping photos

To crop a photo:

1   In the toolbar, select the Crop Overlay tool to enter crop view. When you do, a boundary appears around the border of the photo with resize handles. Also, the toolbar shows additional cropping options, as shown in Exhibit 3-16.

2   Do any of the following:
   - Drag the resize handles to set the crop boundary you want. As you drag, the Rule of Thirds grid is visible. You can also click the aspect ratio lock to maintain the aspect ratio of the photo.
   - Select the Crop Frame tool and drag on the photo to set a new crop boundary.
   - Choose a preset crop size from the aspect ratio list.

3   If necessary, drag the photo within the crop boundary to position it the way you want.

4   Press Enter or double-click within the crop boundary to crop the photo.

5   If you want to remove the crop settings, click Clear.

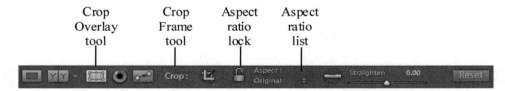

*Exhibit 3-16: Cropping tools in the Develop module toolbar*

### The Rule of Thirds

The *Rule of Thirds* is a principle of composition used by artists and photographers. Lightroom applies a grid overlay that consists of two sets of evenly spaced horizontal and vertical lines. These lines create four intersections similar to the example in Exhibit 3-17. The idea behind the principle is that you should position the photo subject where the lines intersect rather than centered in the frame. For example, in a landscape photo, placing the horizon along an upper or lower horizontal line helps create a well-composed photo. For portraits, placing the subject matter where lines intersect produces a more compelling photo.

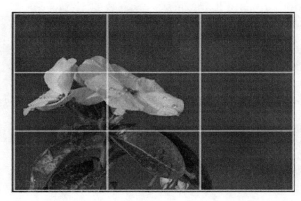

*Exhibit 3-17: A photo showing a Rule of Thirds overlay*

Some cameras include a Rule of Thirds grid that can be turned on and viewed on the LCD. If you don't achieve this layout with a camera, you can apply the principle when cropping the photo in Lightroom. It's also important to mention that there can be exceptions to this rule. There are compelling photos that don't follow this principle.

*Do it!*

## E-1:   Cropping photos

| Here's how | Here's why |
|---|---|
| 1  Use the Filmstrip to select photo DSC_4736 |  |
| 2  In the toolbar, click  | (The Crop Overlay tool.) To enter crop view. A boundary appears around the edges of the photo. |
| 3  Collapse the right panel group | To see the additional cropping options in the toolbar. You've decided that this photo might look good as a panorama. |
| 4  Slowly begin dragging the bottom-center handle up | As you drag, the Rule of Thirds grid is visible. |
| Position the horizon on the lower grid line |  |
| | This adjustment crops out the bottom part of the photo, which appears darkened. You like the aspect ratio, but would prefer that more of the water appear at the bottom. |

5 Drag the photo up until it appears approximately as shown

6 Press ⏎ ENTER

To exit crop view and display only the finished cropped photo.

7 Use the Filmstrip to select photo DSC_3896

This photo has been selected to run full-page in an 8.5×10.5-inch publication. You'll crop it for that purpose.

8 Select the Crop Overlay tool

To enter crop view.

9 In the toolbar, from the Aspect ratio list, select **Enter Custom...**

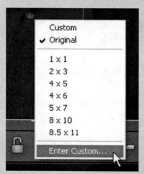

To open the Enter Custom Aspect Ratio dialog box.

In the two fields, enter **8.5** and **10.5**

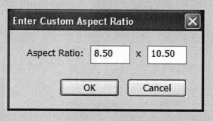

Click **OK**

To set the aspect ratio you entered. You'll use the crop gridlines to apply the rule of thirds.

10  Drag the top-left resize handle
down until the top gridline
approximately aligns with the
man's eyes, as shown

You'll position one of the man's eyes at a
gridline.

11  Drag the photo to position the grid
over the man's eye, as shown

12  Press ( ↵ ENTER )

To exit crop view and display only the finished
cropped photo.

### Straightening

*Explanation*

To straighten a photo:

1  In the toolbar, select the Crop Overlay tool to enter crop view.

2  Do one of the following:

- Point just outside one of the resize handles until the rotate icon is visible; then drag to rotate the photo.

- Select the Straighten tool, shown in Exhibit 3-7, and drag in the photo to create a line. The line indicates the angle you want to rotate the photo. For example, in a photo of a landscape, drag to create a line along the horizon to indicate how much to rotate the photo. You can also temporarily select the Straighten tool by pressing and holding Ctrl.

- In the toolbar, drag the Straighten slider. Dragging to the right rotates the photo clockwise. Dragging to the left rotates the photo counter-clockwise. The straighten angle shows the angle of rotation.

3  Press Enter, or double-click within the crop boundary to straighten the photo.

*Exhibit 3-18: Straightening options in the Develop module toolbar*

When you straighten a photo, Lightroom automatically crops it in order to maintain the aspect ratio and prevent empty space from showing at any edge.

*Do it!*

### E-2:  Straightening photos

| Here's how | Here's why |
|---|---|
| 1  Use the Filmstrip to select photo DSC_4736 again | The cropped landscape photo. |
| 2  In the toolbar, click | (The Crop Overlay tool.) To enter crop view. |

3  Point above the top-right resize handle, as shown

To access the rotation pointer.

Drag slightly up to rotate the photo until the horizon is parallel with one of the gridlines that appears

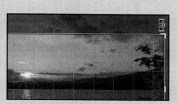

4  In the toolbar, observe the angle value

The negative number indicates that you rotated the photo slightly counter-clockwise.

Press ⏎ ENTER

To exit crop view and display the cropped photo.

5  Use the Filmstrip to select photo DSC_4334

You'll use the Straighten tool to correct this horizon.

6  In the toolbar, click the Crop Overlay tool

Hold down CTRL

To temporarily select the Straighten tool.

7  Drag from the left side of the horizon (where the water meets land) to the right

When you release the mouse button, the photo rotates to align to the line. It also automatically crops the photo, maintaining the aspect ratio and preventing empty space from showing at any edge.

8  Press ⏎ ENTER

To exit crop view.

# Topic F: Detail adjustments

*Explanation*

You can make detail adjustments to photos, such as sharpening or noise reduction. *Noise* in digital photos consists of any undesirable flecks of random color in a portion of the photo that should consist of smooth color.

## The Detail panel

To make sharpening and noise reduction adjustments, you can use the Detail panel, shown in Exhibit 3-19. The panel consists of two Noise Reduction sliders, Luminance and Color; and a Sharpening section. The Luminance slider reduces grayscale noise, and the Color slider reduces chroma noise.

When you make sharpening and noise reduction adjustments, you should always view the photo at a *minimum* of 1:1 magnification, which provides you with a 100% view of the actual pixels. In the center pane, the visible portion of the photo should correlate to the adjustment you're making. Noise adjustments are more apparent in flat-colored areas. Sharpening adjustments are more noticeable in detailed areas. Also, typically the more you sharpen a photo, the more noise becomes apparent, so often it's good to make sharpening adjustments first.

*Exhibit 3-19: The Detail panel*

*Do it!*

## F-1: Controlling photo detail

| Here's how | Here's why |
|---|---|
| 1 Use the Filmstrip to select photo DSC_3896 | |
| | You'll optimize this photo for sharpness and noise reduction. |
| 2 Expand the right panel group | If necessary. |
| 3 Create a snapshot named **Color original** | |

| | | |
|---|---|---|
| 4 | Click the man's eye | To zoom in. You'll zoom in further so that you can more clearly see the effect of each setting you choose. |
| | In the Navigator panel, select **3:1** | |
| | Reposition the photo so the man's eye is visible | (If necessary.) Each photo pixel is represented by three monitor pixels, so the detail and noise in the photo are very clear. The more you sharpen a photo, the more noise becomes apparent, so you'll maximize the sharpening first. |
| 5 | In the right panel group, scroll down to view the Detail panel | |
| | Under Sharpening, drag the Amount slider to 150 | The detail improves somewhat, but the photo appears grainier. |
| 6 | In the Navigator panel, click the solid-colored ceiling in the background | (To display that area in the center pane.) Noise is most apparent in flat colored areas. |
| 7 | In the Detail panel, under Noise Reduction, drag the Luminance slider to approximately 60 | The noise is significantly decreased. |
| 8 | Create a snapshot named **Sharpen and smooth** | |
| 9 | Set the magnification to **1:1** | To view the photo pixels without further magnification. |
| 10 | In the Navigator panel, click the man's eye | To display that area in the center pane. |
| 11 | Compare the photo's appearance with the two checkpoints, returning to Sharpen and Smooth when finished | Observe the man's eyebrow as you view the checkpoints. |
| 12 | Click in the photo | To return it to Fit magnification. |

# Topic G: Duplicating adjustments

*Explanation*

Earlier you learned how to synchronize photos in the Library module. You can perform the same task in the Develop module. You can also copy and paste adjustments. Both techniques work similarly, but the copy and paste technique provides you with a little more control. You can also create presets in the Develop module with more precision than in other modules. When you create a preset, you can specify which attributes to include.

## Copying adjustments

There are several ways to copy adjustments from one photo and apply them to another:

- If you want to apply all the adjustments from the current photo you've just finished adjusting to another photo, select the new photo in the Filmstrip and click Previous at the bottom of the right panel group. This method applies all adjustments from the previous photo. You do not have control over which adjustments to apply.

- If you want to apply specific adjustments from the current photo, click Copy at the bottom of the left panel group. When you do, the Copy Settings dialog box appears, as shown in Exhibit 3-20. Similar to the Synchronize dialog box, you can check or clear the specific adjustments you want to copy. To apply the adjustments, select a new photo in the Filmstrip and click Paste.

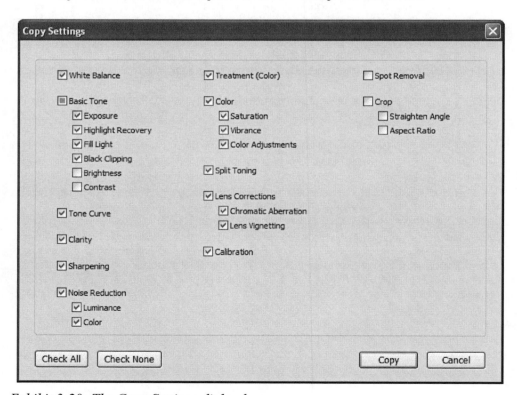

*Exhibit 3-20: The Copy Settings dialog box*

If you have more than one photo selected in the Filmstrip, the Previous button changes to the Sync button, which works the same way as the Sync button in the Library module.

*Do it!*    **G-1:   Copying and pasting adjustments**

| Here's how | Here's why |
|---|---|
| 1  Verify that photo DSC_3896 is still selected | (The photo of the man.) You want to apply the same adjustments you've applied to this photo to another photo of a girl. However, you don't want to include the cropping adjustments. |
| 2  At the bottom of the left panel group, click **Copy...** | The Copy Settings dialog box appears. |
| 3  In the bottom-left corner, click **Check All** | (If necessary.) To check all the adjustment selections. |
| 4  Clear **Crop** | To prevent Lightroom from copying the same cropping adjustments you made to this photo. |
|    Click **Copy** | To close the dialog box. |
| 5  Click the triangle at the bottom of the interface to expand the Filmstrip | So that it stays visible, if necessary. |
| 6  Use the Filmstrip to select photo DSC_4296 |  The photo to the right of the current one. |
| 7  At the bottom of the left panel group, click **Paste** | To paste the color and detail adjustments, but not the crop adjustment.  You'll apply the same adjustments to another photo. |
| 8  Use the Filmstrip to select photo DSC_3903 |  The photo to the right of the current one. |
| 9  At the bottom of the right panel group, click **Previous** | The photo is converted to color and has the same detail adjustments you applied to the previous one. |

# Develop presets

*Explanation*

In addition to copying and pasting adjustments between photos, you can also create presets as a way to duplicate adjustments. Usually, you create presets based on a specific photo you've already adjusted. But sometimes a photo might include some adjustments that you don't want in the preset. In the Develop module, you can specify exactly which adjustments to include.

To create a preset:

1   In the left panel group, in the Presets panel title bar, click the plus sign to open the New Develop Preset dialog box, shown in Exhibit 3-21.

2   Enter a descriptive name in the Preset Name box.

3   Check or clear the settings you want to include or remove from the preset. You can quickly check or clear all the settings by clicking Check All or Check None.

4   Click Create to create the preset.

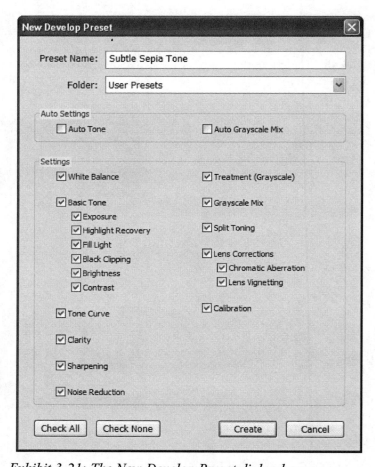

*Exhibit 3-21: The New Develop Preset dialog box*

**Camera calibration and lens corrections**

The right panel group also includes the Camera Calibration and Lens Corrections panels, as shown in Exhibit 3-22. Lightroom uses color profiles for all supported camera models. When you make white balance adjustments, Lightroom uses the profiles to make the color adjustments. Each individual camera—not just camera model, but the specific camera—handles color slightly differently. While Lightroom's profiles may be fairly accurate in general, you might find that photos still tend toward a certain tint. To compensate for this, you can make more precise adjustments in the Camera Calibration panel.

Also, certain lenses you use may tend to create certain distortions, such as *chromatic aberrations*, which are color fringes, particularly at high-contrast edges, and *vignetting*, which is darkening at the outsides of the photo frame. You can use the Lens Corrections panel to make lens adjustments.

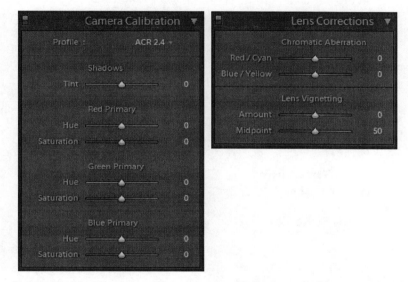

*Exhibit 3-22: The Lens Corrections and Camera Calibration panels*

To retain the adjustments you make in both panels, you can create a preset in the Presets panel. You would then apply the preset to all photos imported from that camera. Because the settings apply only to those two specific areas, you could then further adjust the photo.

*Do it!*

## G-2: Creating a Develop preset

| Here's how | Here's why |
|---|---|
| 1 Use the Filmstrip to select photo DSC_3199 | |
| | (The sepia photo of the clock tower.) You'll create a "Subtle Sepia Tone" preset based upon the split toning adjustment you created for this photo. |
| 2 In the left panel group, scroll up to view the Presets panel | If necessary. |
| 3 On the right side of the panel title bar, click + | To open the New Develop Preset dialog box. |
| In the Preset Name box, enter **Subtle Sepia Tone** | This preset should apply only the Grayscale Conversion and Split Toning adjustments. |
| 4 Click **Check None** | To clear all of the options. |
| Check **Treatment (Grayscale)** | |
| Check **Split Toning** | |
| 5 Click **Create** | To add the preset to the panel. You'll apply the preset to another photo. |
| 6 Use the Filmstrip to select photo DSC_3209 | |
| | The stadium scoreboard photo to the right of the current photo. |
| 7 In the Presets panel, click **Subtle Sepia Tone** | The sepia effect you created for the clock tower is applied to the photo. |

# Unit summary: Developing photos

*Topic A*    In this topic, you applied a **preset** from the Presets panel to a photo. You also adjusted **white balance** in a photo and you made basic tonal adjustments by using Histogram and Basic panels.

*Topic B*    In this topic, you used steps in the History panel to revert a photo to a previous version. You also created **snapshots** of a photo as a way to keep track of previous versions. Lastly, you compared before and after versions of a photo to preview adjustments as you make them.

*Topic C*    In this topic, you made **tonal adjustments** by manipulating a **tone curve** in the Tone Curve panel. You also made precise **shadow and highlight adjustments** by using the Histogram and Tone Curve panels. Lastly, you adjusted the color in a photo by using the HSL/Color/Grayscale panel group.

*Topic D*    In this topic, you converted photos to **grayscale** and adjusted them b y using the Grayscale panel. You also created a **split tone effect** by using the Split Toning panel.

*Topic E*    In this topic, you **cropped** and **straightened** photos by using options in the toolbar.

*Topic F*    In this topic, you made precise **sharpening** and **noise reduction** adjustments by using the options in the Detail panel.

*Topic G*    In this topic, you duplicated adjustments to other photos by copying and pasting them, synchronizing them, and creating **custom presets**.

## Independent practice activity

In this practice activity, you'll adjust several photos within the Develop module. You'll adjust white balance and make tonal adjustments by using a tone curve. You'll also apply the adjustments from one photo to several others. You'll convert a photo to grayscale and colorize it. Lastly, you'll crop and straighten several photos.

1 Use the Filmstrip to select photo DSC_4272 (one of the series of five yellow Labrador photos).

2 Set the white balance by using the Daylight preset. (*Hint:* Select the preset from the WB list in the Basic panel.)

3 Fine tune the white balance by sampling a section of the white fence in the background. (*Hint:* Use the White Balance Selector in the Basic panel. Click a portion of the fence to sample it.)

4 Using the Tone Curve panel, darken the shadow tones in the photo. (*Hint:* Either drag downward on the left side of the curve in the tone graph, or click the Adjust Tone Curve button and drag downward on a dark area in the photo.)

5 Increase the highlight tones in the photo. (*Hint:* Either drag upward on the right side of the curve in the tone graph, or click the Adjust Tone Curve button and drag upward on a light area in the photo.)

6 Use the region sliders to continue fine-tuning the tone curve. (*Hint:* Drag the region sliders left or right to increase or decrease the tonal areas affected by the Shadow and Highlights sliders.

7 Create a snapshot titled **Adjusted highlights and shadows**.

8 Add two more dog photos to the selection and apply the same white balance and tonal range settings you established for the first photo. (*Hint:* Use the Sync command to apply the settings.)

9 Use the Filmstrip to select photo DSC_4296. (*Hint:* The photo is of a girl in a pink striped shirt.)

10 Convert the photo to grayscale. (*Hint:* In the HSL/Color/Grayscale panel title bar, click Grayscale.)

11 Using the Grayscale panel, fine tune the contrast and tonal range of the photo. (*Hint:* Switch back to a color version of the photo to see the dominant colors; then switch to grayscale and adjust the color sliders in the panel.)

12 Lightly colorize the photo by using the Split Tone panel. Make the highlight tones a yellow color, and the shadow tones a dark brown color. (*Hint:* Press Alt as you drag the Hue sliders to see the hue color before you adjust the saturation.)

13 Create a new preset titled **Yellow/brown split tone** for the split tone effect. Include only the split tone adjustments in the preset. (*Hint:* Click + in the Presets panel title bar. In the dialog box, clear everything except the Split Toning option.)

14 Crop the photo using 8.5×11-inch crop dimensions. Position the girl's right eye so that it is along the top line of the rule of thirds grid. (*Hint:* Click the Crop Overlay button in the toolbar, then select 8.5×11 in the list. Resize the crop overlay to position the girl's eye with the top gridline. Part of the girl might be cropped out of the picture. Press Enter to accept the crop changes.)

15 Use the Filmstrip to select photo DSC_0628. (*Hint:* It's one of the daylight beach photos.)

16 Straighten the photo so that the horizon is level. (*Hint:* Click the Crop Overlay button in the toolbar. Press Ctrl to temporarily select the Straighten tool; then drag along the horizon line to straighten the photo. Press Enter to accept the changes.)

## Review questions

1 Which are ways you can adjust white balance? (Choose all that apply.)

   A  Select a white balance preset in the Basic panel.

   B  Use the Highlights slider in the Tone Curve panel.

   C  Select the White Balance Selector tool and click an area in a photo.

   D  Right-click a light area in the photo and choose Set White Balance.

2 Which statements about histograms are true? (Choose all that apply.)

   A  A histogram is a graphical representation of the tonal range of a photo.

   B  If a photo's histogram does not extend all the way to the left or right in the Histogram panel, the photo does not contain a full tonal range and usually has weak contrast.

   C  The left side of a histogram represents lighter pixels, the right side represents darker pixels, and the center represents midtone pixels.

   D  You can make adjustments to a histogram by dragging within the Histogram panel.

3 How can you make adjustments to a tone curve? (Choose all that apply.)

   A  Drag up or down in the tone curve graph.

   B  Click the Adjust Tone Curve button in the Tone Curve panel; then drag directly on the photo.

   C  Adjust the sliders in the Tone Curve panel.

   D  Double-click an area in a photo and drag up or down to adjust the tone curve.

4 True or false? The sliders in the HSL and Color panels produce similar results, but they organize the sliders in different ways.

5 True or false? By using the Split Tone panel, you can apply two colors to a grayscale photo—one color for shadows and one for highlights.

6 Which is the best way to copy all the adjustments from one photo to another?

   A  Select the adjusted photo and click Copy. In the dialog box, verify that all the options are checked and click Copy. Select another photo and click Paste.

   B  Select both photos and click Sync. In the dialog box, verify that all the options are checked and click Synchronize.

   C  Select the photo you want to apply the adjustments to and click Previous.

   D  Right-click the adjusted photo and choose Copy Settings; then right-click the photo you want to adjust and click Paste Settings.

# Unit 4

## Slideshows

**Unit time: 60 minutes**

Complete this unit, and you'll know how to:

**A** Preview a slideshow, adjust basic slide and backdrop options, and save custom slideshow settings as a template.

**B** Add text overlays to slides and adjust the size and placement of photos.

**C** Adjust playback options for a slideshow and export a slideshow as a PDF.

# Topic A:  Slide and backdrop settings

*Explanation*

To begin creating a slideshow, select a series of photos and switch to the Slideshow module. It's common to select photos and make adjustments before you begin assembling a slideshow, but you can also specify photos by using the Filmstrip from within the Slideshow module. After you've selected the photos you want to include, you can preview the slideshow, make basic slide and backdrop adjustments, and even save custom settings as a template.

## Preview slideshows

As you work on a slideshow, you'll likely want to preview it periodically to make sure the changes you're making appear the way you intended in the final output. You can preview a slideshow in the center pane by clicking the slideshow controls in the toolbar, shown in Exhibit 4-1. You can also preview a fullscreen rendition of a slideshow by doing one of the following:

- At the bottom of the right panel group, click Play.
- Choose Slideshow, Run Slideshow.
- Press Enter.

Go to first slide
Go to previous slide
Go to next slide
Preview Slideshow

*Exhibit 4-1: Slideshow controls*

When a slideshow reaches the last photo, a message appears indicating that it will repeat itself, and it returns to the first photo again. To exit a slideshow preview, press Esc or click one of the slides. You can also pause a slideshow by pressing P.

### Impromptu Slideshow command

You can also preview a series of photos as a slideshow in other modules. This is useful if you've already created a slideshow, but want to make further photo adjustments. To preview a slideshow in other modules, choose Window, Impromptu Slideshow or press Ctrl+Enter.

## Adjust photo order

One of the most basic changes you'll likely perform for a slideshow is changing the photo order. You can do this by dragging the photos to the left or right in the Filmstrip. When you drag a photo, a white line appears between two of the other photos to indicate the photo's new position, as shown in Exhibit 4-2.

*Exhibit 4-2: Changing the photo order in the Filmstrip*

## The Template Browser

You can make adjustments for a slideshow by using the panels in the right panel group. However, Lightroom also includes predesigned templates in the Template Browser panel in the left panel group, shown in Exhibit 4-3. You can preview the templates by pointing to them and observing the changes in the Navigator panel. To apply a template, click one in the list.

*Exhibit 4-3: The Template Browser panel*

### A-1: Viewing a basic slideshow

| Here's how | Here's why |
|---|---|
| 1 Switch to the Library module | If necessary. (Press G or click Library in the upper-right corner of the interface.) |
| 2 In the Collections panel, select **Natural beauty article** | You'll create a slideshow to display these photos. |
| 3 Switch to the Slideshow module | (Press Ctrl+Alt+3, or click Slideshow in the top-right corner of the interface.) There are several ways to preview a slideshow. |
| 4 At the bottom of the right panel group, click **Play** | A full screen rendering of the photos begins playing starting with the first photo. After a few seconds the next photo appears, and so on. |
| When the first image reappears, press (ESC) | To stop the slideshow. You can also preview a slideshow within the center pane. |
| 5 In the toolbar, click | (The Preview Slideshow button.) This time the slideshow plays within the center pane. |
| Press (ESC) | To stop the slideshow. You'll change the photo order. |
| 6 In the Filmstrip, drag the arctic fox photo to the left of the waterfall photo until a black line appears, as shown | |
| When the black line is visible, release the mouse button | The arctic fox photo is now before the waterfall photo. |
| 7 Move the photo of the child on the beach to the right of the last flower photo | Drag the child photo to the right until a black line appears; then release the mouse button. |
| 8 In the toolbar, click | (The Go to first slide button.) To select the first photo. You'll experiment with the templates that came with Lightroom. |
| 9 In the left panel group, in the Template Browser panel, expand **Lightroom Templates** | |
| Point to each template name | In the Preview panel, the photo size, background color, and text vary from template to template. |
| Select **Exif Metadata** | The background is set to black, and basic information appears around the edges of the slide. |

| 10 | Preview a full screen rendering of the slideshow | Click Play in the right panel group. |
| --- | --- | --- |
|  | Press ( ESC ) | To stop the slideshow. |

## Slide options

*Explanation*   Other adjustments you can make to a slideshow include zooming to fill the entire frame, changing the stroke border, or applying and adjusting cast shadows. You can make these adjustments by using the Options panel at the top of the right panel group, shown in Exhibit 4-4.

*Exhibit 4-4: The Options panel*

By default, the Zoom to Fill Frame option is cleared. If you check it, Lightroom stretches the photo to fit entirely within the current page guides. Depending on the dimensions of the photo, this could result in some of it being cut off. However, this also provides a good way to ensure that all the photos appear the same size, should you want them to be.

Lightroom also applies a default border and cast shadow. To adjust the cast shadow, use the sliders and the angle wheel in the Cast Shadow section, shown in Exhibit 4-4. To change the stroke border color, click the color swatch to the right of the Stroke Border option. Use the Width slider to increase the stroke width.

*Do it!*

## A-2: Adjusting slide options

| Here's how | Here's why |
|---|---|
| 1 In the Template Browser panel, select **Default** | To return the slideshow back to its default settings. You'll make adjustments from this starting point. You'll start by changing the border color. |
| 2 In the right panel group, in the Options panel, click the color swatch to the right of Stroke Border | |
| | To open the Color dialog box. |
| Under Basic Colors, click the black color swatch | |
| Click **OK** | |
| 3 Drag the Width slider to 5 px | To increase the stroke width. |
| 4 Under Cast Shadow, drag the Opacity slider to approximately 65% | To make the shadow darker. |
| 5 Drag the Offset slider to approximately 65 px | The photo's shadow moves further out. |
| 6 Drag the Radius slider to approximately 70 px | The photo's shadow is feathered, giving it more depth. |

### Backdrop settings

You can make adjustments to the slideshow backdrop by using options in the Backdrop panel, shown in Exhibit 4-5. The *backdrop* refers to the screen area outside the boundaries of the photo. You can create and adjust a color wash, apply a background image, or change the background color. A *color wash* is a gradient of two colors; the color you select for the color wash and the color of the background.

*Exhibit 4-5: The Backdrop panel*

*Do it!*

## A-3:   Adjusting backdrop settings

| Here's how | Here's why |
|---|---|
| 1  In the right panel group, scroll down to view the Backdrop panel | By default, a color wash is already established. You'll adjust it to make it more prominent. |
| 2  In the panel, click the color swatch to the right of Background Color | To display the Color dialog box. You'll add a bit more contrast to the default color wash. |
| Drag the Luminance slider up until the Lum value is approximately 200 | To increase the brightness of the background color. |
| Click **OK** | |
| 3  In the panel, click the color swatch to the right of Color Wash | To open the Color dialog box. |
| Drag the Luminance slider down until the Lum value is approximately 60 | To darken the color wash color. |
| Click **OK** | |
| 4  Drag the Angle wheel until the Angle value is approximately 145 degrees, as shown | The darker color now starts in the upper-left corner, and the color wash fades to the lighter color in the lower-right corner. |

## Templates

*Explanation*

If you want to apply the same slideshow settings to other groups of photos, you can save the settings as a template in the Template Browser panel. To create a template, click the Add button at the bottom of the left panel group, below the Template Browser panel.

You also might want to add new adjustments to a template, after you've already created it. To do this, make the adjustments you want, right-click the template title in the Template Browser panel, and choose Update with Current Settings.

*Do it!*

### A-4: Creating slideshow templates

| Here's how | Here's why |
|---|---|
| 1  At the bottom of the Template Browser panel, click **Add** | To open the Edit dialog box. |
| Type **Dark color wash** and press ( ↵ ENTER ) | |
| 2  Preview the slideshow | (Click Play in the right panel group or press Enter.) |
| | You like the basic appearance but want to change the angle of the color wash. |
| Press ( ESC ) | To return to the Slideshow module. |
| 3  In the Backdrop panel, adjust the color wash angle to approximately 180 degrees | |
| 4  In the Template Browser panel, right-click **Dark color wash** | |
| Select **Update With Current Settings** | To change the definition of the template you created. |

# Topic B: Slide overlays and layout

*Explanation*

After you've set basic slide and backdrop options, you might want to add other elements to your slides, such as an identity plate, or text and rating overlays. You also might want to adjust the size and layout of the photos.

## Identity plates

You can personalize the interface with custom identity plates. The default identity plate is the Adobe Photoshop Lightroom logo in the upper-left corner of the interface. You can replace the logo with either personalized text or a graphic showing your identity or company logo. Identity plates can be a nice touch if you are presenting work to clients using Lightroom. They are also useful when creating slideshows or web galleries, and for printing. You can create multiple identity plates, if necessary, and then select them when you need them.

To create an identity plate:

1 Choose Edit, Identity Plate Setup to open the Identity Plate Editor shown in Exhibit 4-6.

2 Do one of the following:

- In the left box, enter personalized text for the plate. You can format the text by using the Font, Type Style, and Type Size lists below the box.

- If you want to import a graphic to use for the plate, click the Use a graphical identity plate radio button above the box. When you do, the box changes to show a preview for the graphic. Click Locate File to navigate to the graphic you want to use, and then click Open to import it.

3 In the upper-left corner, check Enable Identity Plate to replace the default Adobe plate with the text or graphic you specified. The new identity plate becomes visible in the upper-left corner of the interface.

4 Click OK to close the dialog box.

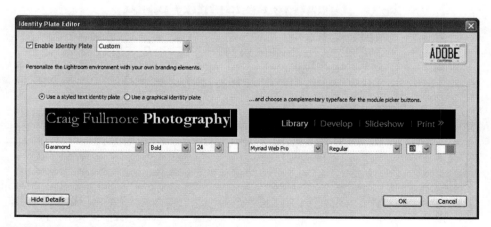

*Exhibit 4-6: The Identity Plate Editor*

### Font color

You can change text color for textual identity plates by selecting the text and clicking the small color swatch, shown in Exhibit 4-6. Doing so opens the Color dialog box, shown in Exhibit 4-7. You can use the dialog box to select basic colors or create custom colors by using the color spectrum, the color value boxes, and/or the Luminance slider.

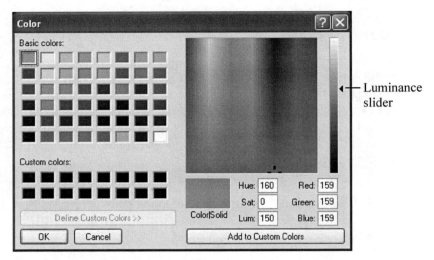

Exhibit 4-7: The Color dialog box

### Module bar adjustments

You can adjust the text used to trigger modules in the upper-right corner of the interface by using the options on the left side of the dialog box, as shown in Exhibit 4-6. This is optional, but can provide a good way to ensure that the module picker text complements the text you might have selected for textual identity plates. You can hide these additional options by clicking Hide Details in the lower-left corner.

*Do it!*

## B-1: Creating an identity plate

| Here's how | Here's why |
|---|---|
| 1 Choose **Edit,** **Identity Plate Setup...** | To open the Identity Plate Editor. By default, the text box has the text "Lightroom." You'll update that with your name. |
| 2 Type **<Student Name> Photography** | To replace the existing text. (Type your name for the text inside the brackets.) |
| | The text uses the default font and size of the previous text, so depending on the length of your name, the text might not all be visible. You'll alter the dialog box to be able to manipulate the text, if necessary. |
| 3 In the bottom-left corner, click **Hide Details** | To hide the module bar options and make the dialog box narrower. |

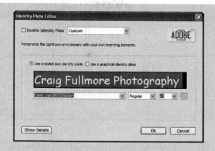

4  Drag the right side of the dialog box to the right

To make it wider so that all the text is visible.

5  Format the text by using the Font and Type Size lists

Select any font you like. Set the type size at approximately 26 pt.

6  Double-click the word **Photography**

To select just the word.

From the Type Style list, select **Bold**

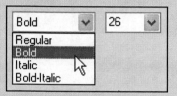

(If possible.) You'll also make the selected text white.

7  On the right side, click the gray color swatch

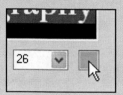

To open the Color dialog box.

Under Basic colors, click the white color swatch and click **OK**

To change the color. You'll now replace the default Lightroom identity plate with the text you've established.

8  In the upper-left corner, check **Enable Identity Plate**

In the upper-left corner of the interface, the default Lightroom identity plate is replaced with the formatted text.

9  Click **OK**

To close the dialog box.

## Add Identity plates

*Explanation*

To add an identity plate to a slideshow, use the Identity Plate options in the Overlays panel, shown in Exhibit 4-8. If you've already created an identity plate for the interface, it will automatically be active in the panel and visible in the upper-left corner of the slide. You can reposition the identity plate within the slide, and make basic adjustments to it.

You can also create custom identity plates by clicking the preview in the panel, and choosing Edit from the drop-down list to open the Identity Plate Editor.

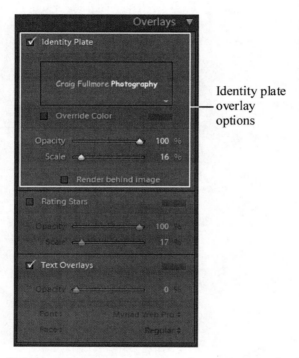

Identity plate overlay options

*Exhibit 4-8: Identity plate overlay options in the Overlays panel*

### Manipulate identity plates

If you choose to include an identity plate, you can position, scale, or rotate the plate in the slideshow. The plate will appear on all slides, so it does not matter which slide is visible when you position and adjust it. To manipulate an identity plate overlay, do any of the following:

- To adjust plate size, drag one of the bounding box handles. If the plate consists of text, the text size is increased. If the plate uses a graphic, the size of the graphic is increased. Be careful when enlarging graphic plates, as it can cause the graphic to distort.

- To move the plate, point to the plate so that the pointer changes to a hand, and then drag the plate where you want it. As you move the plate, it tethers itself to points on the photo's border or to the edges of the slide. This allows the plate to float next to photos or within photos at a consistent distance, regardless of the size or orientation of the photos.

- To rotate a plate, click the rotate buttons in the toolbar.

*Do it!*

## B-2: Adding an identity plate

| Here's how | Here's why |
|---|---|
| 1 In the Overlays panel, observe the Identity Plate options | You'll reposition and adjust the plate within the slideshow. |
| 2 Use the Filmstrip to select the portrait waterfall photo | |
| | You'll use this photo to position and resize the identity plate because the size of the plate will affect this photo the most. |
| | To make it easier to work with the slideshow, you'll collapse the left panel group and the Filmstrip. |
| 3 Collapse the left panel group and the Filmstrip | (Click the small triangles on the left side and bottom of the interface.) The slide preview in the center pane is much bigger. |
| 4 In the upper-left corner of the slide, point to the identity plate text | The pointer changes to a hand. |
| 5 Slowly begin dragging the text down and to the right | As you drag, the text shifts to tether itself to different areas of the slide and photo. |
| Position the text near the lower-left corner of the photo, as shown | |
| | Be sure the text is tethered to the lower-left corner of the photo. |
| 6 Point to the upper-right box handle | |
| | The pointer changes to two arrows pointing in opposite directions. |
| 7 Slowly drag up and the right | To increase the size of the text. As you drag, the Scale option in the Overlay panel increases. |
| Scale the identity plate to approximately 35% | In the Overlay panel, you can see the Scale slider move and its value increment. |

8 In the Overlay panel, drag the Opacity slider to approximately 75%

9 Click a blank area of the slide

To deselect the identity plate.

10 In the toolbar, click

(The Go to next slide button.) To advance to the next slide in the slideshow. For landscape photos, the identity plate automatically positions itself in the lower-left corner the same way it did in the portrait photo.

# Text overlays

*Explanation*

To add text or rating overlays to your slides, use the options in the Overlays panel shown in Exhibit 4-9. By default, Lightroom enables text overlays. To view photo ratings, check Rating Stars. You can also adjust the color, size, and opacity of rating stars.

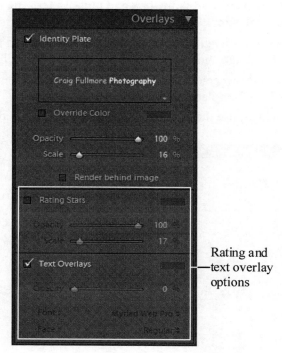

*Exhibit 4-9: Rating and text overlay options in the Overlays panel*

**Text overlays**

To add text to slides:

1 In the toolbar, click the Add text to slide button. When you do, a text box automatically appears in the toolbar to the right of the button.

2 Do one of the following:

- Enter the text you want in the box and press Enter. The text you enter will appear on each slide.

- Click the small triangles to the right of the text box and select a metadata tag from the list. Each slide will show the metadata for each photo.

- To specify other metadata information, choose Edit from the text box list to open the Text Template Editor, shown in Exhibit 4-10.

3 To format the text, use the options under Text Overlays in the Overlays panel.

*Exhibit 4-10: The Text Template Editor*

To edit existing text overlays, select the text overlay and then choose Edit from the text box list in the toolbar. After you've added a text overlay, you can position, scale, or rotate the text similar to the way you manipulated the identity plate.

**The Text Template Editor**

Within the Text Template Editor, you can specify text strings to display different types of metadata. For example, you can add metadata tags that will automatically show the file name for each photo, as well provide a brief description. To add metadata, expand one of the lists in the panel and select a metadata tag from the list, or click Import next to a metadata tag that is already visible. Each list is categorized for specific metadata types. You can add multiple metadata tags as well as mixing metadata and custom text. Metadata tags are separated by brackets, as shown in Exhibit 4-10.

*Do it!*

## B-3: Adding text overlays

| Here's how | Here's why |
|---|---|
| 1 Use the Filmstrip to select the portrait waterfall photo again | (If necessary.) You'll have to expand the Filmstrip temporarily to select the photo. |
| 2 In the Overlays panel, clear **Identity Plate** | To hide the identity plate. |
| | The photo's file name appears by default beneath the photo. You'll edit this to display other information. |
| 3 Select the file name text overlay beneath the photo | |
| | Click the text to select it. |
| 4 In the toolbar, from the Custom Settings list, choose **Edit...** | To open the Text Template Editor dialog box. |
| 5 Under IPTC Data, to the right of the Copyright option, click **Insert** | To add the Copyright metadata tag to the box at the top. |
| 6 Click **Done** | The new text is very small, so you'll make it bigger. |
| 7 Point to the top-center handle of the text box, as shown | |
| | Until two arrows appear pointing in opposite directions. |
| Drag up slowly | To increase the size of the text. Make sure the length of the text will fit within the width of the photo. You'll also adjust the font and color. |
| 8 In the Overlays panel, under Text Overlays, from the Font list, select **Arial Black** | |
| 9 To the right of Text Overlays, click the black color swatch | |
| | To open the Color dialog box. |
| Under Basic colors, click the white color swatch and then click **OK** | You'll also position the text on the lower-left corner of the photo. |

10 Position the text in the lower-left corner of the photo

(Point to the text until a hand icon is visible; then drag to move the text. Be sure the text is tethered to the lower-left corner of the photo, not the slide.) You'll add another text overlay at the bottom-right corner of the slide.

11 In the toolbar, click

(The Add text to slide button.) A text box appears to the right of the button in the toolbar.

In the box, type
**No reproduction without prior permission**

Press ( ↵ ENTER )

To insert the text in a field within the slide.

12 Resize and position the text as shown

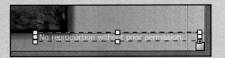

Use the resize handles to adjust the size of the text. When you position it, be sure the text is tethered to the lower-right corner of the slide.

13 Click a blank area of the slide

To deselect the text box. You'll now preview some of the slides.

14 Using the controls in the toolbar, advance forward through the slideshow

For landscape photos, the copyright text overlay automatically positions itself in the lower-left corner the same way it did in the portrait photo.

# Layout

*Explanation*
To adjust the position of photos in a slideshow, you use the options in the Layout panel, shown in Exhibit 4-11. The photo position relies on four guides; Left, Right, Top, and Bottom. By default, all four guides are linked. If you adjust one of the guides, it affects the other guides the same way to ensure photos are always centered. Sometimes though, you might want to adjust guides individually. To unlink the guides, click Link All at the bottom of the panel to deselect it. You can also link two or more guides by clicking the small boxes to the left of the sliders.

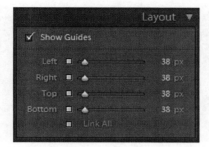

*Exhibit 4-11: The Layout panel*

You can adjust guides either by dragging them in the center pane (shown in Exhibit 4-12) or by adjusting the sliders in the Layout panel. You can also specify an exact position for guides by clicking the pixel value to the right of the sliders and entering a new value.

*Exhibit 4-12: Positioning photos by using the guides*

## B-4: Adjusting guides

| Here's how | Here's why |
|---|---|
| 1 Use the Filmstrip to select the portrait photo of the waterfall | (You'll have to temporarily expand the Filmstrip to select the photo.) The rights usage terms you added at the bottom of the slide appears much closer to the portrait orientation photo than to the landscape ones. You'll adjust the bottom margin to minimize this issue. |
| 2 In the center pane, point to the bottom guide | |
| | Until a double-headed arrow appears. |
| 3 Slowly drag the guide up | As you drag the guide, all the guides shift inward. You want to adjust only the bottom guide, so you'll need to unlink the guides. |
| 4 In the right panel group, scroll to view the Layout panel | If necessary. |
| 5 To the left of the Bottom slider, click the small box | |
| | To unlink the bottom guide from the others. |
| 6 Set the bottom guide at approximately 50 px | You can either drag the guide or drag the Bottom slider. |
| 7 Set the Left guide at approximately 38 px | (Again, you can either drag the guide or drag the Left slider.) Because the Left, Right, and Top guides are still linked, all three reflect the change. |
| 8 Use the controls in the toolbar to advance to the beach-scene slide | The left, top, and right edges of the landscape photo are very close to the edges of the slide, making it look cramped. |
| 9 In the center pane, drag the top guide down | To shrink the size of the photo. Because the bottom guide is still unlinked, it remains stationary. |
| Adjust the guides so that the photo looks less cramped on the slide | |
| 10 Create a new template named **Natural Beauty** | You'll have to temporarily expand the left panel group. At the bottom of the panel group, click Add, enter the name, and click OK. |

11  Use the Filmstrip to select the portrait photo of the waterfall

You decide that the portrait orientation for this slide might be a distraction, so you'll make each photo fill the entire space within the guides.

12  In the Options panel, check **Zoom to Fill Frame**

(The Options panel is at the top of the right panel group.) The photo is enlarged to fill the guide boundaries, which means some of it is now being cut off at the top and bottom.

Drag the photo up or down as necessary

So that it looks suitable within the guides. You decide that it might be best to display the photos at full screen, with no guides.

13  In the Layout panel, click **Link All**

To link all the guides again.

14  Click one of the guide values, as shown

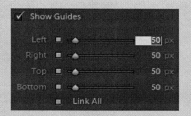

To make it active.

Enter **0** and press ⏎ ENTER

To eliminate the space outside the photo.

15  Create another template named **Natural Beauty Fullscreen**

16  Preview a fullscreen version of the slideshow

(Press Enter.)

When you are finished previewing, return to the Slideshow module.

# Topic C: Playback and export settings

*Explanation*

After you've finalized the slides in a slideshow, you can adjust some of the playback settings and export it so that others can open it.

### The Playback panel

Some playback options you can adjust include the length of time the slides are visible, the transition speed between slides, whether or not to add music, and whether or not the slides are randomized. These options are available in the Playback panel, shown in Exhibit 4-13.

*Exhibit 4-13: The Playback panel*

*Do it!*

### C-1: Choosing playback settings

| Here's how | Here's why |
|---|---|
| 1 In the right panel group, scroll down to view the Playback panel | You'll make the slides linger for more time and slow down the slide transitions. |
| 2 Drag the Slides slider to a value of 5.0 sec | |
| Drag the Fades slider to a value of 3.0 sec | |
| 3 Preview a fullscreen version of the slideshow | The slides appear at a more relaxed pace than before. When you are finished, return to the Slideshow module. |

## Slideshow output

*Explanation*

When you've completed a slideshow, you can either play it within Lightroom as a way to present your work, or export it in PDF format to distribute it to others.

To export a slideshow:

1   Verify that you're in the Slideshow module.
2   Press Ctrl+D to verify that no slides are selected. If a slide is selected, Lightroom will export only that slide, and not the entire slideshow.
3   At the bottom of the right panel group, click Export to open the Export Slideshow to PDF dialog box, shown in Exhibit 4-14. You can also choose Slideshow, Export Slideshow or press Ctrl+J. You can use the dialog box to specify a descriptive name and location for the slideshow and to adjust the quality and size.
4   Click Save to export the slideshow.

*Exhibit 4-14: The Export Slideshow to PDF dialog box*

A slideshow exported as a PDF requires viewers to use Acrobat Reader in order to open it. Acrobat Reader is very common, and those who don't have it can download it for free from the Adobe website (www.adobe.com).

### Export options

It's important to understand the options in the Export Slideshow as PDF dialog box. For example, the Quality slider controls photo quality. A higher setting generates higher-resolution photos, but also increases the file size of the PDF. A lower setting creates lower resolution slides, and thus a smaller file size. In general, you'll want a higher setting so that people see your work at its best. However, a lower setting is useful if you need to send the slideshow via e-mail, or if you want to post it online.

The Width and Height boxes determine the width and height of the background for the slideshow. By default, the values reflect your current monitor resolution. If you intend to share your slideshow with a lot of people, you might want to set the values to a commonly used monitor resolution, such as 800×600, or 1,024×768.

The Automatically show full screen option instructs Acrobat Reader to present the slideshow in fullscreen mode when it's opened. This can enhance the impact of your slideshow because viewers will automatically see your work at full screen instead of being presented with the first slide within Acrobat Reader.

*Do it!*

## C-2: Viewing and exporting slideshows

| Here's how | Here's why |
|---|---|
| 1 At the bottom of the right panel group, click **Export...** | To open the Export Slideshow as PDF dialog box. |
| 2 Navigate to the Slideshows subfolder | In the current unit folder. |
| 3 In the File name box, enter **Natural Beauty** | You won't be emailing or posting this version of the slideshow online, so you'll increase the photo quality. |
| 4 Drag the Quality slider to 100 | You'll also set the size of the background to a common monitor resolution. |
| 5 In the Width box, enter **1024** | If necessary. |
| In the Height box, enter **768** | (If necessary.) Lastly, you'll set the slideshow so that it automatically opens in full screen mode. |
| 6 Check **Automatically show full screen** | |
| 7 Click **Save** | To generate the slideshow document in PDF format. In the upper-left corner of the interface, in place of the identity plate, you can see the progress Lightroom makes as it exports the slideshow. |
| 8 In Windows Explorer, navigate to the Slideshows subfolder | In the current unit folder. |
| Double-click **Natural Beauty.pdf** | To open the file and play the slideshow automatically in Adobe Reader. |
| When the slideshow is finished, press ( ESC ) | |
| 9 Exit Adobe Reader | |
| 10 Activate Lightroom | If necessary. |

# Unit summary: Slideshows

**Topic A**   In this topic, you previewed a basic slideshow by using several techniques. You also adjusted the **stroke** and the **cast shadow** and created a **color-wash background**. Lastly, you saved custom slide settings as a **template** in the Template Browser panel.

**Topic B**   In this topic, you added text and **rating overlays** to slides. You also used **guides** to position and crop photos against the background.

**Topic C**   In this topic, you made basic playback adjustments, such as slide and **transition** duration. You also exported a final slideshow as a **PDF**.

## Independent practice activity

In this activity, you'll create a slideshow template for the band Sprocket with specific layout and display options.

1 In the Library module, in the Collections panel, select the Band photos collection. Then switch back to the Slideshow module. (*Hint:* Press G to switch to the Grid view in the Layout module.)

2 Using the Template Browser, apply the Default slideshow template.

3 Using the Filmstrip, rearrange the photos to any sequence you want. (*Hint:* You'll have to expand the Filmstrip to see it.)

4 Remove the default stroke border and cast shadow. (*Hint:* Change the settings by using the Options panel.)

5 Create a solid light-brown background color. (*Hint:* Create the background color by using the Backdrop panel. In the Color dialog box, we used Red: 115, Green: 85, and Blue: 51. To remove the color wash, clear Color Wash.)

6 Use the guides to offset the photos near the lower-left corner of the background, similar to the example in Exhibit 4-15. (*Hint:* Use the Layout panel to adjust the guides. We set the guides at Left: 395 px, Right: 45 px, Top: 110 px, and Bottom: 35 px.)

7 Check the **Zoom to Fill Frame** option so that Lightroom fills the guides with the photos. Scan through the slides and reposition the photos within the guides, if necessary. (*Hint:* The Zoom to Fill Frame option is in the Options panel.)

8 Add a custom text adornment with the text **Sprocket**, and **May 2006 Recording Session**. Format and position the text similar to the example in Exhibit 4-15. You can use any fonts available on your computer. (*Hint:* You can edit any existing text adornments if any exist on the slide.)

9 Set the slide duration to 2.5 seconds, and the transition duration to 0.5 seconds. (*Hint:* Use the Playback panel to make the adjustments.)

10 Preview the slideshow and export it as a high-quality PDF.

*Exhibit 4-15: One of the slides in the final slideshow*

## Review questions

1 Which are ways to preview a slideshow? (Choose all that apply.)

A At the bottom of the right panel group, click Play.

B Press Enter.

C Double-click the slide in the center pane.

D In the toolbar, click the Play button.

2 How can you adjust the order of slides in a slideshow?

3 Which panel allows you to adjust slide borders and cast shadows?

A Layout panel

B Options panel

C Backdrop panel

D Overlays panel

4 How can you adjust the size of a text overlay?

A In the Text Overlays section in the Overlays panel, drag the Text Size slider.

B Drag one of the bounding box handles.

C Right-click the text and choose a preset size.

D Double-click the text and choose a preset size.

5 How can you export a slideshow? (Select all that apply.)

A At the bottom of the right panel group, click Export.

B Press Ctrl+J.

C Choose File, Export Photos.

D Choose Slideshow, Export Slideshow.

# Unit 5

## Printing photos

**Unit time: 60 minutes**

Complete this unit, and you'll know how to:

**A** Adjust the way photos are arranged on pages, including single photo layouts and multiple photo layouts.

**B** Adjust output settings, including basic printing options and color management options.

# Topic A: Print layout

*Explanation*

To print a photo or series of photos, select the photos you want to print and switch to the Print module. Like the Slideshow module, you can adjust and categorize photos prior to switching to the Print module, but you can also specify photos to print directly by selecting them in the Filmstrip.

## Basic print settings

When you switch to the Print module, Lightroom is configured by default to print photos individually. You can verify this by observing the single preview in the center pane and the number of pages in the toolbar. For example, if you selected six photos, the first photo is visible in the center pane, and the toolbar shows 1 of 6, as shown in Exhibit 5-1.

The default view also shows basic page setup options in the upper-left corner, which consists of the page you're currently viewing, the paper size, and the printer. Sometimes this information can be distracting because it overlaps the photos, so you can toggle off and on by pressing I. Rulers are also visible to the left and top of the page preview, which match the current page size.

 — Navigation buttons

*Exhibit 5-1: The default view in the Print module*

After you've selected photos to print, you'll likely want to change some of the default printing settings. To change page layout, you can choose from templates in the Template Browser panel. You can also select a printer, and page sizes and orientation from the Print Setup dialog box, shown in Exhibit 5-2. To open the Print Setup dialog box, click Page Setup in the toolbar, or click Print Settings in the right panel group.

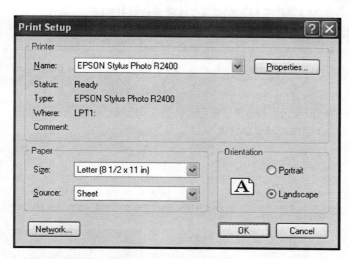

*Exhibit 5-2: The Print Setup dialog box*

If you set options in the Print Setup dialog box, selecting one of the default templates can change the page orientation, but the page size you select will always remain intact. To navigate between pages, click the navigation buttons in the toolbar.

*Do it!*

## A-1: Adjusting basic print settings

| Here's how | Here's why |
|---|---|
| 1 Switch to the Library module | (If necessary.) Press G, or click Library at the top-right corner of the interface. |
| 2 In the Collections panel, select **Natural beauty article** | If necessary. |
| 3 Press CTRL + A | To select all the photos in the collection. |
| 4 Switch to the Print module | Click Print in the top-right corner of the interface, or press Ctrl+Alt+4. |
| 5 Observe the toolbar at the bottom of the center pane | Page 1 of 6 |
| | When you first display a collection in the Print module, each photo will print on its own sheet. |
| 6 Click ➡ | (The Show next page button.) To view the second photo in the collection. |
| 7 In the Filmstrip, click the last photo | To select it. |
| 8 Observe the toolbar | Page 6 of 6 |
| 9 In the toolbar, click ▢ | (The Show first page button.) To return to the first page. You'll now select a printer and adjust page size and orientation. |
| 10 In the toolbar, click **Page Setup...** | To open the Print Setup dialog box. |
| 11 From the Name list, select **EPSON Stylus Photo R2400** | (If necessary.) To select a printer capable of printing large, high-quality color and black and white photos. You'll set up printing on standard letter size paper. |
| 12 Under Paper, from the Size list, verify that **Letter (8 1/2 x 11in)** is selected | |
| From the Source list, verify that **Sheet** is selected | Because most of these photos use landscape orientation, you'll set the printer orientation to match. |
| 13 Under Orientation, select **Landscape** | |
| Click **OK** | The information in the upper-left corner reflects the changes, and the photos are set to landscape orientation. |

| | |
|---|---|
| 14 Observe the rulers above and to the left of the photo | The rulers match the paper size (8 1/2 × 11). If you apply a template, the page orientation could change (depending on the template), but the page size you select will always remain intact. |
| 15 In the Template Browser panel, select **Fine Art Mat** | Under Lightroom Templates. The paper orientation changes back to portrait, but the rulers indicate the paper is still set as 8 1/2 × 11. |
| 16 In the toolbar, click **Page Setup...** | To open the Print Setup dialog box. You'll change the paper size and then apply another template. |
| From the Size list, select **Super B (13 x 19 in)** | |
| Click **OK** | The photo and ruler dimensions increase, but the Fine Art Mat template is still selected in the Template Browser panel. |
| 17 In the Template Browser panel, select **4 Wide** | To apply another template. Four of the photos are visible on the sheet, but the page size remains at 13 ×19. |
| 18 Press ( *I* ) | To hide the overlay information in the upper-left corner. |

## Page layout

*Explanation*

So far, you've made basic layout adjustments by using templates and the options in the Print Setup dialog box. But you can more precisely adjust page layout by using the options in the Layout panel, shown in Exhibit 5-3.

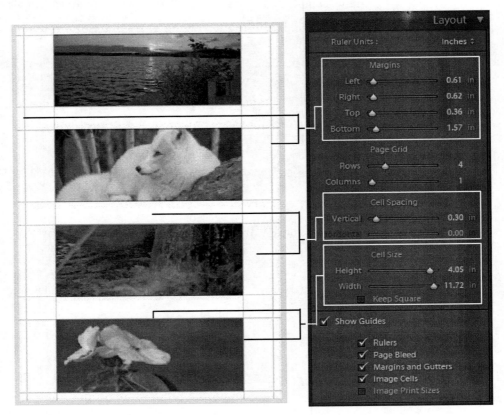

*Exhibit 5-3: An example of page layout showing four rows and one column*

As you make adjustments by using the panel, it's important to understand that some options are linked to others, depending on the type of layout you are working with. For example, in a layout that consists of multiple photos, adjusting the margins will likely also adjust cell size and spacing. You might need to experiment to obtain the exact adjustments you want.

### Margins

The Margin sliders position a photo or photos relative to the page edges. Enlarging the margins may cause cell sizes and spacing to shrink. This often depends on the page size you're working with. For example, on 13-inch tall paper, you can print an 11-inch tall cell with top and bottom margins each set to 1 inch (11 + 1 + 1 = 13). If you increase the top margin to 2 inches, the cell size must decrease to 10 inches to accommodate the large margin.

### Page Grid

The Page Grid sliders control the number of rows and columns in a layout. If you increase the number of rows or columns, the cell size and spacing sliders automatically adjust to accommodate the additional photos.

### Cell Spacing and Cell Size

The Cell Spacing sliders determine the amount of space between each photo in a multi-photo layout. Often, increasing the cell spacing between photos will automatically adjust their cell size. Again, this depends on the exact layout you're working with and the size of the paper. The Cell Size sliders determine the size of the photo or photos in the layout. No photo may exceed the cell size.

### Manipulating photos in a multi-photo layout

You can also adjust layouts to print multiple copies of photos. To do so, check Repeat One Photo per Page in the Image Settings panel. This instructs Lightroom to fill all the cells on each page with one photo. The number of pages in the toolbar increases to match the number of photos you're printing.

*Do it!*

## A-2: Setting up a multi-photo layout

| Here's how | Here's why |
|---|---|
| 1 In the right panel group, scroll down to view the Layout panel | You'll decrease the width of the photos by adjusting the cell size width. |
| 2 Under Cell Size, drag the Width slider slowly to the left | As you drag, the width of the photos begins to decrease on both the left and right sides. |
| Set the cell width to approximately 8 in | You'll also separate the pictures a little more. |
| 3 Under Cell Spacing, drag the Vertical slider slowly to the right | As you drag, the height of the photos begins to decrease. You don't want the heights to change; you just want to add more space between the photos. |
| Drag the slider back to 0.30 in | To undo the change. |
| 4 In the Layout panel, observe the Margins | The 4-Wide template you applied earlier set the bottom margin to 1.57 inches. This setting is preventing you from adding any cell spacing. |
| 5 Under Margins, click the value to the right of the Bottom slider, as shown | |

| Here's how | Here's why |
|---|---|
| | To select the value. |
| Type **.36** and press ( ↵ ENTER ) | The adjustment spreads the photos evenly down the page. |
| 6 Observe the toolbar | Because there are six photos, there are two pages to print. |
| 7 In the toolbar, click ▶ | (The Show next page button.) To view the second page. The page shows the last two photos. |
| In the toolbar, click ◀ | To return to the first page. You decide to print multiple copies of each photo. |
| 8 In the Image Settings panel, check **Repeat One Photo per Page** | The same photo appears in all four cells on the page. |
| 9 Observe the toolbar | The toolbar now indicates that there are six pages, one page for each photo. |
| 10 Click ▶ | To view the second page. |

## Fitting photos to cells

*Explanation*

In some situations, photos might not fit within cells the way you intended. For example, if the dimensions of a photo don't match the dimensions of the cell, there will be white space above and below, or to the right and left of the photo, as shown in Exhibit 5-4.

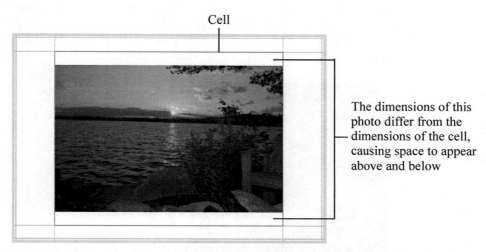

*Exhibit 5-4: An example of a photo in which the dimensions differ from the cell*

If the photo dimensions differ from the cell dimensions, you can force the photo to fill the cell entirely by checking Zoom to Fill Frame in the Image Settings panel. The photo retains its aspect ratio, but parts of the photo are cropped outside the boundaries of the cell. You can reposition the photo in the cell by dragging it left or right, or up and down.

**Overlays**

If you want to include information about photos when you print them, you can add information by using the options in the Overlays panel, shown in Exhibit 5-5. You can add an identity plate, page option information, and basic photo metadata. Photo metadata appears within the photo cell, which can change the size of the photo. In general, photo metadata is more useful for layouts such as contact sheets, where the exact size of the photo on the page isn't critically important. Page Options attributes appear near the page edge inside the gutter (the non-printable area for that combination of printer and properties).

*Exhibit 5-5: The Overlays panel*

*Do it!*

## A-3: Setting up a specific size print

| Here's how | Here's why |
|---|---|
| 1 Display the arctic fox photo | |
| 2 In the Template Browser panel, select **Maximize Size Centered** | (To reset the page dimensions so that the photos fill the page.) You decide you want to print fullsize versions of the photos. Because most of these photos are of landscape orientation, you'll change the paper orientation to match. |
| 3 In the toolbar, click **Page Setup...** | To open the Print Setup dialog box. |
| Select **Landscape** | |
| Click **OK** | You'll create a layout for an 11×14-inch print. |
| 4 In the Layout panel, under Cell Size, click the value to the right of the Height slider | Cell Size<br>Height 12.71 in<br>Width 18.76 in<br>Keep Square |
| Type **11** and press ↵ ENTER | |
| 5 Use the same technique to set the cell width to 14 | (Click the value to the right of the Width slider, type 14, and press Enter.) This photo has a wider aspect ratio than the cell, so there is white space at the top and bottom. As of now, the photo would print 14 inches wide, but only about 9 inches tall. |
| 6 In the Image Settings panel, check **Zoom to Fill Frame** | (You might need to scroll up in the right panel group to see the panel.) The photo enlarges to fill the entire cell. You can adjust the position of the photo within the cell, because some is now cropped out on the left and right sides. |
| In the center pane, drag the photo as desired to position it within the cell | You can only drag horizontally, because the vertical dimension is automatically fit to the cell. |
| | You want the photo positioned a bit higher on the paper for the purpose of matting. |
| 7 In the Layout panel, under Margins, drag the Bottom slider to a value of approximately 3 inches. | To move the photo up on the page. |

8 Under Cell Size, observe the Height value

With the large bottom margin, the photo can no longer print at 11 inches tall on 13 inch tall paper. You'll reduce the bottom margin to allow for a cell height of 11 inches.

Under Margins, drag the Bottom slider to a value of approximately 1.4 inches

The cell height value returns to 11 inches.

9 In the Overlays panel, check **Photo Info**

You might need to scroll down to view the panel.

Click the Custom Settings control and select **Filename**

If necessary.

10 Clear and check **Photo Info** a few times, observing the effect on the photo's size

The photo prints slightly smaller when Photo Info is displayed. Because you want a specific size print, you'll turn off photo information.

11 Clear **Photo Info**

12 Check **Page Options**

13 Check options as shown

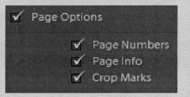

(If necessary.) This information appears outside the cell border, so it doesn't reduce the size of the photo.

### Templates

*Explanation*

You can save custom layouts as templates in the Template Browser panel in the left panel group. Unlike the default templates, any custom templates you create affect page size as well as page orientation.

To create a custom template:

1   Configure the layout you want for the template.
2   At the bottom of the left panel group, beneath the Template Browser panel, click Add.
3   Enter a descriptive name for the template and click OK.

*Do it!*

## A-4:   Saving settings to a template

| Here's how | Here's why |
|---|---|
| 1   Below the Template Browser panel, click **Add** | To create a new template. |
| In the Name box, enter **11 x 14 inch landscape** and press (⏎ ENTER) | You'll verify that applying the template controls the paper size as well as the page orientation. |
| 2   Press (I) | To show the overlay information in the upper-left corner. |
| 3   In the toolbar, click **Page Setup...** | To open the Print Setup dialog box. |
| Under Paper, from the Size list, select **Letter (8 1/2 x 11 in)** | |
| Under Orientation, select **Portrait** | |
| Click **OK** | The paper size and orientation change. |
| 4   In the Template Browser panel, click **11 x 14 inch landscape** | To apply the template you created. The paper size and orientation return to 13×19 and landscape. |
| 5   Press (I) | To hide the overlay information again. |

## Automatic rotation

*Explanation* The photos you want to print might vary in orientation (landscape vs. portrait). If you are printing any overlay information, this could cause the text to print along the side of some photos and at the bottom of others. Depending on the photos, you can sometimes prevent this by deselecting the Auto-Rotate to Fit option in the Image Settings panel. This prevents photos from automatically rotating to fit the layout, as shown in Exhibit 5-6. However, it can also cause some of the photo to be cropped outside the boundaries of the cell. In general this option is effective only if the photos you are working with can be cropped adequately.

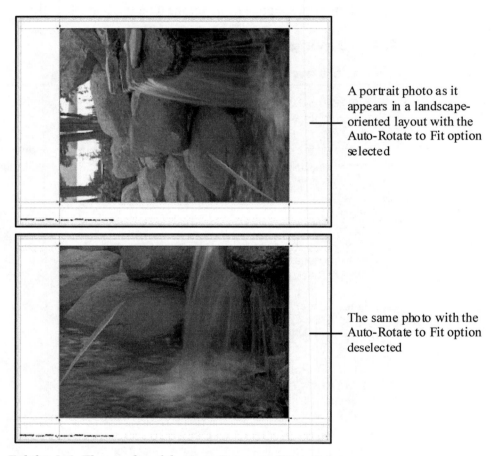

A portrait photo as it appears in a landscape-oriented layout with the Auto-Rotate to Fit option selected

The same photo with the Auto-Rotate to Fit option deselected

*Exhibit 5-6: The results of the Auto-Rotate to Fit option*

*Do it!*    **A-5:    Rotating prints**

| Here's how | Here's why |
|---|---|
| 1  Use the Filmstrip to select the waterfall photo | Because this is a portrait photo, it is displayed sideways. However, you want to rotate the photo so that the photo information is at the bottom of the photo, not to the side. |
| 2  In the Image Settings panel, clear **Auto-Rotate to Fit** | To force this photo to print with a landscape aspect ratio. Some of the photo is cropped in order to fit within the cell. |
| Verify that Zoom to Fill Frame is checked | |
| Drag to center the photo in the cell | (If necessary.) While this photo doesn't look as good in landscape format, the others may appear reasonable when cropped to portrait format. |
| 3  Open the Print Setup dialog box | In the toolbar, click Page Setup. |
| Under Orientation, select **Portrait** | |
| Click **OK** | The bottom page margin you applied earlier is now visible for the left margin. |
| 4  In the Layout panel, set the left margin to **.12 in** | Click the value to the right of the Left slider, enter .12, and press Enter. |
| 5  In the Filmstrip, select each photo and center them in the cell | Drag the photos to center them. |
| 6  Save a template named **11 x 14 inch portrait** | At the bottom of the Template Browser panel, click Add, enter the name for the template, and click OK. |

### Borderless printing

*Explanation*

It's not uncommon to want to print *borderless* photos, or photos that bleed off the edge of the paper. Borderless printing saves you from having to trim them after printing them. To print borderless prints, you must use a printer that supports borderless printing.

In Lightroom, you need to set the margin guides to zero and the cell size needs to match the exact size you want to print to. Most SLR (single-lens reflex) cameras create photos with a 3:2 aspect ratio, in which the width of a landscape picture is 1.5 times the height. This matches 4×6-inch photo prints. Most consumer digital cameras create pictures with a 4:3 aspect ratio, in which the width is 1.33 times the height. This is closer to matching other common print sizes, such as 8×10 and 5×7, because those prints are closer to square than are 4×6 prints.

If you want to print a photo on paper stock that doesn't match its aspect ratio, you must check Auto-Fill to Frame in the Image Settings panel to force the photo to fit the cell. You can then drag the photo to choose which part to crop when printing.

*Do it!*

### A-6: Setting up borderless prints

| Here's how | Here's why |
|---|---|
| 1 Open the Print Setup dialog box | (In the toolbar, click Page Setup.) You'll set up borderless printing on 4×6-inch paper. |
| | This printer can print borderless only on certain papers, so you must choose properties to specify one that will work. |
| Click **Properties...** | (To open the EPSON Stylus Photo R2400 Properties dialog box.) You'll print to glossy photo paper. |
| 2 Under Paper & Quality Options, from the Type list, select **Premium Photo Paper Glossy** | |
| 3 From the Size list, select **4 x 6 in** | |
| 4 Check **Borderless** | (To specify edge-to-edge printing.) A dialog box appears explaining that the print quality near the edges may decline on borderless prints. |
| Click **OK** | To dismiss the warning dialog box. |
| 5 Under Orientation, select **Landscape** | |
| Click **OK** | To close the EPSON Stylus R2400 Properties dialog box. |
| Click **OK** | To close the Print Setup dialog box. To print borderless, you must set the margin guides to zero. |

6  In the Overlays panel, clear **Page Options**

To eliminate the text at the bottom of the print.

7  In the Layout panel, set the Left, Right, Top, and Bottom margins to zero

To eliminate any margins. The cell size needs to match the exact size you want in order for the photo to print edge-to-edge.

8  Under Cell Size, drag the Height and Width sliders all the way to the right

To increase the values to exactly 4 and 6 inches. The photo now fills the entire size of the page with no gutter or margins.

9  In the Filmstrip, select the photo of the waterfall

(If necessary.) You'll rotate photos automatically for printing borderless to avoid cropping pictures like this.

In the Image Settings panel, check **Auto-Rotate to Fit**

To match this photo's orientation to the page.

10  Save a template named **4 x 6 inch landscape borderless**

At the bottom of the Template Browser panel, click Add, enter the name for the template, and click OK.

# Topic B: Output control

*Explanation*

When you've established the layout you want, you can make printing adjustments by using the Print Job panel. Lightroom provides a range of printing options depending on what your intentions are for your prints. You can print rough, low-quality draft prints as well as high-quality, color-managed prints.

## Basic print settings

By default, Lightroom sets photo resolution at 240 dpi (dots-per-inch), which is adequate for most photos. Some very detailed photos might benefit from printing with a resolution of around 300 dpi. You can adjust printing resolution by changing the value in the Print Job panel, shown in Exhibit 5-7. You can also enhance sharpening by using the Print Sharpening list.

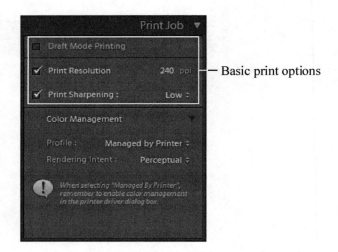

*Exhibit 5-7: Basic print options in the Print Job panel*

Sometimes you might want to print low-quality versions of photos. For example, if you wanted to print a quick contact sheet, or a draft of a photo for review. If you check Draft Mode Printing, Lightroom sends thumbnail data to the printer, which creates lower quality output but usually dramatically speeds up printing time.

To print photos, click Print at the bottom of the right panel group and choose File, Print, or press Ctrl+P.

*Do it!*

## B-1: Choosing basic print settings

| Here's how | Here's why |
|---|---|
| 1  In the Template Browser panel, click **11 x 14 inch landscape** | To prepare for printing the photos at a large size. |
| 2  In the Right panel group, scroll down to view the Print Job panel | Because these photos are larger, you'll increase the resolution some. |
| 3  In the panel, click the value to the right of Print Resolution<br><br>Type **300** and press ⏎ ENTER | To select it. |
| 4  Verify that Print Sharpening is checked | You'll make the sharpening a bit more aggressive. |
| 5  From the sharpening strength list, select **Medium** | |

## Color management

*Explanation*

If you are printing high-quality photos, you can also use color management to help ensure the colors in your photos print the way you intended. There are two ways you can do this. You can either let Lightroom color manage your prints, or let the printer color manage your prints.

### Color management within Lightroom

If you decide to color manage your prints within Lightroom, you need to be sure you have the most current ICC profile(s). Usually, the printer profile is included when you first install the printer driver for your printer. Periodically, however, printer manufacturers will update printer profiles or offer specific printer/paper profile combinations and offer them as free downloads. For example, you can download specific profiles for your printer that target the type of paper you are using (glossy, semi-glossy, and so on). You can usually locate them on the printer manufacturer's Web site.

To manage color within Lightroom, you need to work with the color management options in the Print Job panel, shown in Exhibit 5-8. If you downloaded specific profiles, you'll need to select the one you want to use in the Profile list. You'll also need to choose a rendering intent, which controls how out-of-gamut colors are rendered to colors the printer can duplicate.

In Lightroom, you can select either Perceptual or Relative.

- Perceptual rendering tries to visually preserve the contrasting differences in colors. However, in doing this, it might change in-gamut colors as well. Perceptual rendering is a good choice when your photo has many out-of gamut colors.

- Relative rendering preserves all in-gamut colors and renders out-of-gamut colors to the closest matching in-gamut color. It preserves more of the original color, but can also result in loss of contrast if there are a lot of out-of-gamut colors.

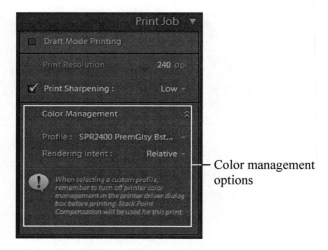

— Color management options

*Exhibit 5-8: Color management options in the Print Job panel*

**Deactivating color management for the printer**

If you choose to manage color in Lightroom, you need to deactivate any default color management settings for your printer; otherwise, your photos could be "color managed" twice, and the colors might not print the way you intend. The method to do this depends on the printer you're using.

*Do it!*

## B-2: Printing with Lightroom-controlled color management

| Here's how | Here's why |
|---|---|
| 1 In the Print Job panel, under Color Management, from the Profile list, select **Other...** | To specify which color management profiles should appear in the list. |
| 2 Check options as indicated | |

| | To display one premium glossy paper profile (PremGlsy), one luster paper profile (PremLuster), one semi-glossy paper profile (PremSmgls) in Lightroom's profile list. |
|---|---|
| | You're intending to print your photos to glossy paper. |
| Click **OK** | |
| 3 Expand the Profile list again | To verify that the profiles you selected are now in the list. |
| 4 From the list, select **SPR2400 PremGlsy BstPhoto.icc** | To set Lightroom to convert photo colors into the color space for that specific printer and paper combination when printing. |
| 5 Navigate through the photos, looking for colors you'd expect to be out of a printer's gamut | These photos don't contain extremely bright, saturated colors that would clearly fall outside a photo printer's gamut. |
| 6 From the Rendering Intent list, select **Relative** | (If necessary.) This rendering intent works well for most photos in which few colors are outside the print gamut. |
| | When Lightroom controls color via a custom profile, you must turn off color management control in the printer driver to avoid "double converting" the image color values. |
| 7 Open the Print Setup dialog box | In the toolbar, click Page Setup. |

| | | |
|---|---|---|
| 8 | Click **Properties** | To open the EPSON Stylus Photo R2400 Properties dialog box. |
| | Click **Advanced** | (If necessary.) To access the color management settings. |
| | Click **Continue** | (If necessary.) On Note window. |
| 9 | Under Color Management, select **ICM** | To indicate that printing is taking place using Windows ICM technology. |
| | Check **Off (No Color Adjustment)** | To prevent the printer driver from adjusting the photo colors. |
| 10 | At the bottom of the dialog box, verify that Show this screen first is checked | To avoid a warning dialog box in the future. |
| | Click **OK** | To close the EPSON Stylus R2400 Properties dialog box. |
| | Click **OK** | To close the Print Setup dialog box. |

## Printer-based color management

*Explanation*

Some default printer drivers do an exceptional job at creating prints, at times exceeding the quality of a custom profile. This may be the case for printers with specialized ink sets. For example, the K3 ink system in the Epson R2400 is optimized for black and white printing, and its printer driver's Advanced Black and White mode typically creates better output than you'd get using a custom profile, because that profile can't map directly to the specialized inks. To allow the printer to manage color, you need to select Managed By Printer in the Profile list. If you previously deactivated color management for the printer, you need to reconfigure it by using the Print Setup dialog box.

*Do it!*    **B-3:    Printing with printer-controlled color management**

| Here's how | Here's why |
|---|---|
| 1  Press Ⓖ | To display the photos in grid view in the Library module. |
| In the Library panel, click **All Photographs** | |
| 2  Select the second black Labrador photo | |
| Convert the photo to grayscale | In the Quick Develop panel, from the Saved Preset list, select General - Grayscale. |
| 3  Switch back to the Print module | Press Ctrl+Alt+4 or click Print in the upper-right corner of the interface. |
| 4  In the Print Job panel, from the Profile list, select **Managed by Printer** | (If necessary.) When you choose to let the printer manage color, you must choose appropriate settings in the Print Setup dialog box to get the desired results. |
| 5  Open the Print Setup dialog box | |
| From the Name list, choose **Epson Stylus Photo R2400** | |
| 6  Click **Properties** | To open the EPSON Stylus Photo R2400 Properties dialog box. |
| 7  From the paper type list, select **Premium Photo Paper Glossy** | |
| 8  From the print quality list, select **Best Photo** | |

Paper & Quality Options

| Sheet ▾ | ☐ Borderless |

Premium Photo Paper Glossy ▾

Best Photo ▾

| 9  Under Color Management, select **Advanced B&W Photo** | |
| Click **OK** | To close the Epson Stylus Photo R2400 Properties dialog box and return to the Print dialog box. |
| Click **OK** | To close the Print Setup dialog box. |

# Unit summary: Printing photos

*Topic A*      In this topic, you adjusted the way photos are prepped for printing. You created both single and multiple **photo layouts**, including rotating and cropping photos, setting up borderless prints, and saving custom layouts as templates.

*Topic B*      In this topic, you set specific **output options**, including basic printing settings, and **managing color** both within Lightroom and using a specific printer.

## Independent practice activity

In this activity, you'll prepare a series of photos for borderless printing on 8½×11-inch paper. You'll also manage color within Lightroom.

1 Switch to the Library module, select the photos in the Band photos collection, and switch back to the Print module. (*Hint:* Be sure to select the photos in the collection to ensure that they'll print.)

2 Apply the Maximize Size template. Set the paper size to 8½×11 inches. (*Hint:* Set the paper size by using the Print Setup dialog box.)

3 Open the Page Setup dialog box and configure the settings necessary for borderless printing. (*Hint:* Click Properties. Select glossy paper and check Borderless.)

4 If necessary, set the margins and cell size to create borderless prints. (*Hint:* Set the margins to 0 [zero] and the cell size to 8½×11.)

5 The photo is a different size than the cell, creating white space above and below. Force the photo to fit the cell size. (*Hint:* In the Image Settings panel, check Zoom to Fill Frame.) Adjust each of the photos, if necessary, so they are centered appropriately.

6 Save the settings in a new template titled "Borderless 8½×11 inches." (*Hint:* Click Add at the bottom of the left panel group.)

7 You'll color manage the photos within Lightroom. You're going to print the photos on semi-glossy paper. Set the appropriate printer/paper profile. (*Hint:* In the Print Job panel, select SPR2400 PremSmglsBstPhoto.icc.)

8 Turn off color management for the printer. (*Hint:* In the Print Setup dialog box, click Properties. Under Color Management, select ICM. Then check Off (No Color Adjustment).

# Review questions

1 How can you toggle the page setup information in the upper-left corner of the center pane?

   A  Press Tab.

   B  Press I.

   C  Double-click the text.

   D  Right-click the text and choose Hide Page Info.

2 How can you open the Print Setup dialog box? (Choose all that apply.)

   A  In the toolbar, click Page Setup.

   B  At the bottom of the right panel group, click Print.

   C  Double-click the photo preview in the center pane.

   D  At the bottom of the right panel group, click Print Settings.

3 True or false? To print multiple copies of a photo on a page, check Repeat One Photo per Page in the Layout panel.


4 True or false? If the photo dimensions differ from the cell dimensions, you can force the photo to fill the cell entirely by checking Zoom to Fill Frame in the Image Settings panel.


5 True or false? You can use any printer to create borderless prints.


6 True or false? If you choose to manage color in Lightroom, you need to deactivate any default color management settings for your printer.

# Unit 6

## Web galleries

**Unit time: 45 minutes**

Complete this unit, and you'll know how to:

**A** Create a Flash-based web gallery, including adding text, adjusting layout and colors, and adding photo information.

**B** Preview a web gallery and upload it to a host server.

# Topic A: Create a web gallery

*Explanation*

It's common for photographers to need to share their work with clients or to want to showcase their work. A common way to do this is by creating web galleries that include specific sets of photos.

## Gallery types

You can either create HTML-based layouts or Flash-based layouts. HTML-based layouts are viewable in a broad range of browsers, and have a very basic structure to them. Flash-based layouts are more professional looking, but require viewers to have the Flash plug-in installed in their browser in order to view the gallery. However, most browsers have the plug-in by default.

## Templates

There are two approaches you can use to create a web gallery. You can select a gallery type (Flash or HTML) in the Gallery panel and then use the other panels to customize the default layout, or you can select a predesigned template from the Template Browser panel and continue to modify it, if necessary.

The Template Browser panel contains a collection of both HTML and Flash-based template layouts. When you point to template in the panel, a preview of the template layout is visible in the Preview panel. HTML and Flash versions are designated in the lower-left corner of the preview. When you select a template, the preview in the center panel is updated automatically and the panels in the right panel group show options available for the gallery type you selected.

HTML-based layouts arrange photos within a grid, similar to the example in Exhibit 6-1. When you click a photo, a larger version is opened. You can then continue to advance through the photos like a slideshow, or you can return to the grid to select another photo.

*Exhibit 6-1: An example of an HTML-based gallery*

Flash-based layouts show thumbnail photos either at the left side of the window or at the bottom of the window, similar to the example in Exhibit 6-2. You can view larger versions of the thumbnails by clicking them or you can specify to view the photos as a slideshow. With either method, the layout is generated automatically when you export or upload the gallery. You do not need to have a working knowledge of HTML or Flash.

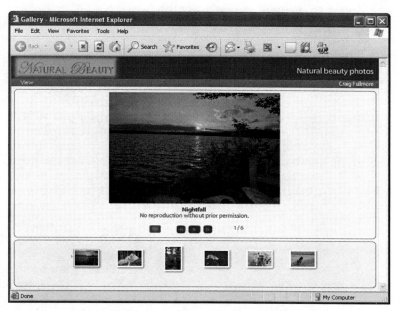

*Exhibit 6-2: An example of a Flash-based gallery*

*Do it!*

## A-1: Creating a basic web gallery

| Here's how | Here's why |
|---|---|
| 1 Switch to the Library module | If necessary. |
| 2 In the Collections panel, select the Natural beauty article collection | |
| 3 Switch to the Web module | (In the upper-right corner of the interface, click Web, or press Ctrl+Alt+5.) |
| 4 In the right panel group, observe the Gallery panel | The panel shows you can create either a Flash-based gallery or an HTML-based gallery. The HTML-based option is selected by default. |
| 5 In the left panel group, in the Template Browser panel, expand **Lightroom Templates** | |
| Point to some of the templates | To preview them in the Preview panel (directly above). As you preview them, the bottom-left corner shows that some are HTML and others are Flash. You want to create a Flash-based gallery. You'll select a Flash template that uses colors that complement some of the colors in the photos. |
| 6 Select **Blue Sky** | The preview in the center pane updates to show the change. Now that you've selected a template, you'll collapse the left panel group, which will provide you with a wider preview. |
| 7 Collapse the left panel group | (Click the small triangle on the left side of the interface.) You'll also collapse the Filmstrip. |
| Collapse the Filmstrip | (Click the small triangle on the bottom of the interface.) The preview now gives you a close representation of how the web page will look when you upload it later. |

## Gallery text

*Explanation*

Once you've selected a gallery type, you can customize it in different ways. For example, you can make basic layout adjustments, change the colors, or update any text. To change or add text, you can use the Site Info panel, shown in Exhibit 6-3. Each field contains default text you can select and change. If you don't want your gallery to include certain types of text, you need to remove the default text.

*Exhibit 6-3: The Site Info panel*

You can also update text by working directly in the preview in the center pane. To do this, click on the text you want to change, as shown in Exhibit 6-4, and enter the new text.

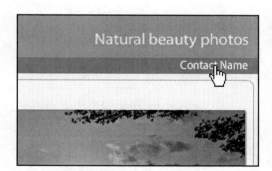

*Exhibit 6-4: Changing text directly in the layout*

*Do it!*

## A-2: Adjusting gallery text

| Here's how | Here's why |
|---|---|
| 1 In the right panel group, observe the Site Info panel | Each label in the panel corresponds to text in the layout. You'll start by updating the site title. You'll be posting the photos on your site. |
| 2 In the Labels panel, in the Site Title box, enter **<Student Name> Photography** and press ⏎ ENTER | Site Title — Craig Fullmore Photography<br><br>In the preview in the center pane, the Site Title text is updated. When you add text to a web gallery, Lightroom saves it as a preset for any other galleries you might create later. |
| 3 Click the small triangle to the right of Site Title, as shown | Craig Fullmore Photography — Site Title — Collection Title<br><br>The text you entered in the box is now available in the list. |
| Click away from the list | To close it. You'll now enter a collection title. |
| 4 In the Collection Title box, enter **Natural beauty photos**, and press ⏎ ENTER | You can also update text directly in the preview. |
| 5 In the center pane, beneath Natural beauty photos, point to Contact Name | Natural beauty photos — Contact Name<br><br>When you point to the text, the pointer changes to a pointing finger and a line appears underneath the text. |
| Click the text | To make it active. |
| Type **<Student Name>** and press ⏎ ENTER | Natural beauty photos — Craig Fullmore<br><br>To update the text. |
| 6 Observe the Contact Info box in the Labels panel | The name you entered is visible. You'll remove any default text that you don't want to include in the gallery. |

7  In the Collection Description box,
    select the default text and
    press ( DELETE )

    Press ( ↵ ENTER )

8  Remove the default text in the          (Select the text in the box and press Delete.
    Web or Mail Link box                    Then press Enter.)

### Customize a web gallery

*Explanation*

The layout adjustments you can make depend on the type of gallery you are working with. If you are working with an HTML-based layout, you can adjust the number of rows and columns used to display the photo thumbnails, as shown in Exhibit 6-5. If you are working with a Flash-based layout, you can select options from the Layout list to control the size of thumbnails and large images. Both gallery types allow you to add an identity plate.

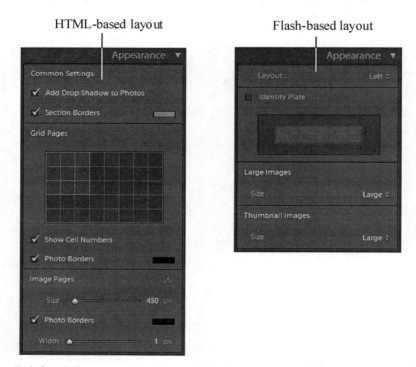

*Exhibit 6-5: Appearance panel options for HTML- and Flash-based layouts*

You can also use the options in the Color Palette panel to adjust the colors, as shown in Exhibit 6-6. To adjust a color, click a color swatch to the right of the layout item you want to adjust. When you do, the Color dialog box appears, within which you can make the color adjustment you want.

*Exhibit 6-6: The Color Palette panel*

*Do it!*

## A-3: Customizing a web gallery

| Here's how | Here's why |
|---|---|
| 1 In the right panel group, scroll down to view the Appearance panel | By default, the gallery has a "scrolling" layout. |
| 2 From the Layout list, select **Left** | 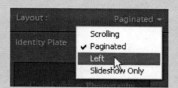 |
| | Now the photo thumbnails are arranged down the left side of the gallery. |
| 3 From the Layout list, select **Scrolling** | The thumbnails are now shown horizontally below the main preview. For this gallery, you'll stick with the scrolling layout. |
| 4 Check **Identity Plate** | The identity plate you created earlier becomes visible in the upper-left corner where the site title text used to be. You have a Natural Beauty logo, so you decide to add that instead of your own identity plate. |
| 5 In the panel, click the identity plate preview and choose **Edit...** |  |
| | To open the Identity Plate Editor. |
| 6 Select **Use a graphical identity plate** | |
| 7 Click **Locate File...** | |
| Navigate to the current unit folder | (If necessary.) |
| Select **Natural Beauty logo.jpg** and click **Open** |  |
| | The graphic appears in the preview pane. |
| 8 Click **OK** | To close the dialog box and add the graphic. The graphic appears in the upper-left corner of the gallery. It has a different color than the color of the title bar, so you'll adjust the site colors. |

9  Scroll up to view the Color Palette panel

You can adjust the color of the title bar by using the color swatch to the right of Header.

10  Click the color swatch to the right of Header

To open the Color dialog box.

11  In the Red, Green, and Blue boxes, enter: 10, 72, and 63, as shown

To create the same color as the logo graphic background. You'll save the color so that you can use it to update other site colors.

12  Click **Add to Custom Colors**

To add the color to the Custom colors section. You'll create another shade of the color to use in the site as well.

13  Drag the Luminance slider up until the Lum value is approximately 80

(Click Add to Custom Colors.)

Add the new color to Custom colors section

14  Under Custom colors, click the darker green color

To select it. (The first color you created.)

15  Click **OK**

Now the title bar matches the background color of the graphic. You'll change the remaining brown colors in the site by using the blue colors you created.

16  Click the color swatch to the right
    of Menu

    Under Custom colors, click the
    lighter green color, as indicated

    To select it.

    Click **OK**                        The light blue bar below the logo is now light
                                        green.

17  Click the color swatch to the right
    of Border

    Under Custom colors, click the
    lighter green color, as indicated

    To select it.

    Click **OK**                        The thin borders dividing up the page are light
                                        green.

18  Click the color swatch to the right    To open the Color dialog box.
    of Text

    Under Custom colors, click the
    darker green color and click **OK**

19  Set the Controls Background color    (Click the color swatch to open the Color dialog
    to the darker green color            box. Under Custom colors, select the darker blue
                                         color and click OK.)

20  Set the Controls Foreground color
    to the lighter green color

### Photo information

*Explanation* It's common to add information to photos in a gallery, such as titles or captions to help describe what viewers are seeing or any other pertinent information. To add photo information, you can use the Image Info dialog box, shown in Exhibit 6-7.

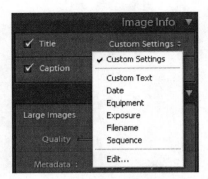

*Exhibit 6-7: The Image Info dialog box*

To add information to photos, do one of the following:

- From the Title or Caption lists, select a metadata type, as shown in Exhibit 6-7. For example, you can select Date or Filename to automatically add the date or file name metadata to the photos.

- Select Custom Text. When you do, a Custom Text box appears beneath the list within which you can enter any text you want.

- Select Edit to open the Text Template Editor dialog box, shown in Exhibit 6-8.You can use the dialog box to specify any type of metadata available in Lightroom. Under each selection, select the metadata type you want and click Insert to add the metadata code at the top. You can also string metadata information together.

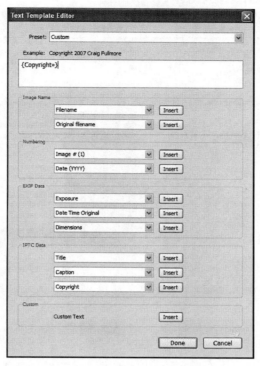

*Exhibit 6-8: The Text Template Editor*

### Presets

If you use the Text Template Editor to add photo information, you can also save the settings you select as a preset, which can make creating future web galleries easier. To create a preset, select Save as New Preset from the Preset list, create a descriptive name for the preset, and click Create. The next time you create a web gallery, you can quickly bring up the same metadata settings by selecting the preset from the Preset list.

*Do it!*

## A-4: Adding information to photos

| Here's how | Here's why |
|---|---|
| 1 In the right panel group, scroll down to view the Image Info panel | (If necessary.) You want the folder name that each photo resides in to be visible. |
| 2 To the right of Title, from the Custom Settings list, select **Edit** | |

To open the Text Template Editor.

| | |
|---|---|
| 3 In the Example box, click **{Title»}** | |

To select the default tag.

| | |
|---|---|
| Press ( *DELETE* ) | To remove it. |
| 4 Under IPTC Data, from the first list, select **Headline** | To add the tag that will automatically add the headline text you created earlier. |
| Click **Done** | Now the headline metadata you created for the photos appears beneath the preview photo in the center pane. |
| 5 In the center pane, click several of the thumbnails | To view the headline text. You'll also add the rights usage terms metadata. |
| 6 In the Image Info panel, to the right of Caption, from the Custom Settings list, select **Edit** | To open the Text Template Editor. |
| 7 In the Example box, click **{Caption»}** | To select the tag. |
| Click the tag a second time | A list appears containing various ITPC metadata you can choose from. |
| 8 From the list, select **Creator Country** | To change the tag. |
| 9 Click **Done** | Now the photographer's country metadata appears beneath the folder names. |

# Topic B: Output a web gallery

*Explanation*

Once you've completed a web gallery, you can either upload it to a server so that others can access it online, or you can export it to a folder to be shared locally. Before you upload or export a gallery, you should preview it in a browser to be sure it looks the way you intended.

## Preview a gallery

To preview a gallery, do one of the following:

- Click Preview in Browser in the toolbar at the bottom of the center pane.
- Click Preview in Browser on the left side of the Output panel title bar.

### Output Settings

You can also make final adjustments to web galleries by using the Appearance panel, shown in Exhibit 6-5, and the Output Settings panel, shown in Exhibit 6-9. When creating a Flash Gallery, the Appearance panel shows settings for determining the size of the preview and thumbnail photos, and the Output Settings shows a slider to control the quality of the photos when they're exported. By default, thumbnails are set as Large, which provides a good-sized view, but can also decrease the size of the Preview photo, especially in Flash-based layouts. To change the size of thumbnails or the preview photo, select a different size from the corresponding lists.

*Exhibit 6-9: The Output Settings dialog box*

You can also decrease the overall file size of a gallery by using the Quality slider. A higher setting produces better-quality photos, but also makes the file size of each photo larger. This can make the gallery load slowly for viewers with a slower Internet connection. You can often reduce photo quality without losing much photo detail onscreen. As you lower the quality setting, you can see the results directly in the center pane. If you are uploading the gallery to a server, it's good to try to achieve the smallest file sizes you can without causing the photos to look bad.

Lastly, you can use the Add Copyright Watermark check box to specify copyright information. If checked, the information is overlayed directly on the lower-left corner of the preview photos.

### Create templates

As with slideshows, you can save a customized gallery as a template in the Template Browser panel. This saves you from having to recreate the gallery layout and colors later on should you want to use it for other photos, and it allows you to use the current layout as a starting point for other layouts. To create a template, click Add at the bottom of the left panel group and enter a descriptive name for the template.

*Do it!*

## B-1: Previewing a web gallery

| Here's how | Here's why |
|---|---|
| 1 In the center pane, observe the gallery layout | Although the preview is smaller than would typically be visible in a browser window, you notice that the thumbnail photos are not much smaller than the preview photo. |
| 2 In the right panel group, observe the Appearance panel | The panel shows settings for determining the size of the preview and thumbnail photos. You'll reduce the size of the thumbnails so that the preview photo will be larger. |
| 3 In the panel, from the Thumbnail list, select **Medium** | |
| | To make the size of the thumbnails smaller. |
| 4 In the Output Settings panel, slowly drag the Quality slider to the left to approximately **65** | In the center pane, the photos are still very clear. Before you preview the gallery, you'll save it as a new template. |
| 5 At the bottom of the left panel group, click **Add** | (You'll need to expand the left panel group to see the button.) |
| Type **Natural Beauty Layout** and press ⏎ ENTER | You'll now preview the gallery in a browser to ensure it looks the way you intended. |
| 6 In the toolbar, click **Preview in Browser...** | In the upper-left corner, you can see the progress Lightroom makes as it temporarily exports the files so that you can preview them. When it finishes, the default browser on your computer opens and the gallery is visible. |
| 7 Expand the browser window | If necessary. |
| 8 Click the thumbnail photos | To view the larger versions. Each time you select a photo, it transitions gradually. |
| 9 In the upper-left corner, click **View** | |
| | To expand the view menu. |
| Select **Slideshow** | The thumbnail photos are removed, allowing viewers to navigate the photos as a slideshow. |

| | | |
|---|---|---|
| 10 | Beneath the main photo, click | To return to the gallery. |
| 11 | Close the browser window | To return to Lightroom. |

## Upload a gallery

*Explanation*

You can either export or upload your galleries. Exporting is useful if you want to share your gallery locally, or if you want to use a specific FTP application to upload the gallery. However, Lightroom does provide basic uploading capabilities as well.

### Upload a gallery

To upload a gallery to a host server, use the options in the Upload Settings panel, shown in Exhibit 6-10. You will need information in order to upload the files, such as the host server address, a user name, and a password. You can get this information from your Internet service provider (ISP). Also, many ISPs have basic uploading information on their Web sites. Many times your user name and password will be the same as your email user name and password settings.

*Exhibit 6-10: The Upload Settings panel*

To upload a gallery within Lightroom:

1 From the FTP Server list, choose Edit to open the Configure FTP File Transfer dialog box, shown in Exhibit 6-11.

2 In the Server box, enter the host server address where you want to upload the gallery.

3 In the Username box, enter the user name. Typically, the hosting center administrator will assign a user name and password.

4 In the Password box, enter your password.

5 If you are uploading to a server in which you already have a hierarchy of folders, you can specify a more specific server path by clicking Browse to the right of the Server Path box. When you do, Lightroom connects to your server and shows the existing folder hierarchy. Navigate to the specific folder you want in the hierarchy and click Select. The file path you chose becomes visible in the box.

6 Click OK to establish the settings.

7 If you want Lightroom to automatically place all files in a subfolder, check Put in Subfolder in the Output panel, as shown in Exhibit 6-10. You can also specify a unique name for the files by entering it in the box below. This is a good option if you are uploading directly to the root site folder, as it keeps the files separate from any other existing files.

8 When you are ready to upload the gallery, click Upload in the bottom-right corner of the right panel group.

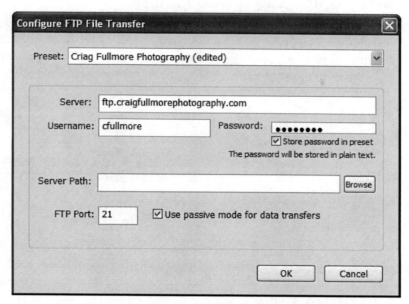

*Exhibit 6-11: The Configure FTP File Transfer dialog box*

## B-2: Uploading a web gallery

| Here's how | Here's why |
|---|---|
| 1  In the right panel group, scroll down to view the Upload Settings panel | (If necessary.) You want to upload the photos to your personal work site from with Lightroom. |
| 2  In the panel, from the FTP Server list, select **Edit...** | |
| | To open the Configure FTP File Transfer dialog box. |
| 3  In the Server box, enter **ftp.<studentname>photography.com** | |
| 4  In the Username box, enter **<student first name>** | |
| 5  In the Password box, enter **password** | You'll save the settings as a preset so that you can upload other galleries without having to re-enter the FTP information each time. |
| Check **Store password in preset** | |
| 6  From the Preset list, select **Save Current Settings as New Preset...** | The New Preset dialog box appears. |
| 7  In the Preset Name box, enter **<Student Name> Photography** | |
| Click **Create** | The name you entered appears in the list. You'll now enter the FTP settings you'll need to access the server. |
| Click **OK** | The preset appears in the FTP Server list in the panel. |
| 8  Click **Upload** | |
| 9  Click **OK** | In the Warning box. |

# Unit summary: Web galleries

**Topic A**    In this topic, you created a Flash-based web gallery. You selected the photos to include in the gallery, added descriptive gallery text, adjusted the gallery layout and colors, and added metadata photo information.

**Topic B**    In this topic, you preview a gallery in a web browser to ensure it looked the way you intended. You also learned how to upload a gallery to a host server by using FTP options within Lightroom.

## Independent practice activity

In this activity, you'll create another web gallery by using a different set of photos. You'll switch templates and then update the template with a new logo, new colors, and a slightly different layout. You'll then preview the final gallery in a browser.

1 Use the Library module to view the Band photos collection; then switch back to the Web module.

2 Use the Template Browser panel to switch to the Warm Day template. (*Hint:* You'll need to temporarily expand the left panel group to see the panel.)

3 Update the Collection Title to "Sprocket band photos." (*Hint:* You can update the text by either typing in the layout or using the Site Info panel.)

4 Activate the default identity plate. (*Hint:* In the Appearance panel, check Identity Plate.) The Natural Beauty logo you used last is visible. You have a Sprocket logo you'll use instead.

5 Replace the current identity plate with Sprocket logo.jpg. The logo is located in the current unit folder. (*Hint:* In the panel, click the identity plate preview and choose Edit to open the Identity Plate Editor.)

6 You'll update the colors in the site, starting with the Header bar. Open the Color dialog box. (*Hint:* In the Color Palette panel, click the swatch to the right of Header.)

7 Create a green color that matches the green background in the logo. The RGB values are 35, 70, and 75. Add the new color to the Custom colors section. Before closing the dialog box, create a second lighter color. Drag the Luminance slider to approximately 100 and add the lighter color to the Custom colors section. Select the darker color again and click OK.

8 Update the remaining colors in the gallery by using the two green colors you created.

9 Observe the layout setting in the Appearance panel. Change layout to "Left."

10 Change the size of the thumbnails to "Medium." (*Hint:* Use the Appearance panel to make the change.) The results should look similar to the example in Exhibit 6-12.

11 Observe the settings in the Output Settings panel. The FTP settings you established for the previous gallery are still active. However, Lightroom automatically updated the Put in Subfolder box. It shows the files will be uploaded to the "Band photos" subfolder. You'll leave the settings as they are.

12 Preview the gallery in a browser. When you're finished previewing, close the browser window to return to Lightroom. (*Hint:* Click Preview in Browser to preview the gallery.)

13 Exit Lightroom.

*Exhibit 6-12: The gallery after completing step 10*

## Review questions

1  What two types of web galleries can you create in Lightroom?


2  Which are ways you can update text in a gallery? (Choose all that apply.)

   A  Enter text in the boxes in the Labels panel.

   B  Select the Text tool, click in the layout, and enter the new text.

   C  Select existing text in the layout and then enter new text.

   D  Double-click in the layout and enter the new text.

3  In which panel can you add photo metadata?

   A  Labels panel

   B  Image Info dialog box

   C  Output Settings panel

   D  Appearance panel

4  Which are ways to preview a gallery? (Choose all that apply.)

   A  In the toolbar, click Preview in Browser.

   B  Click Preview in Browser on the left side of the Output panel title bar.

   C  Press Enter.

   D  Click the gallery controls in the center pane.

# Course summary

This summary contains information to help you bring the course to a successful conclusion. Using this information, you will be able to:

**A** Use the summary text to reinforce what you've learned in class.

**B** Determine the next courses in this series (if any), as well as any other resources that might help you continue to learn about Adobe Photoshop Lightroom.

# Topic A:   Course summary

Use the following summary text to reinforce what you've learned in class.

## Unit summaries

### Unit 1

In this unit, you discussed **Lightroom workflows** and explored the basics of the **Lightroom interface**. You **imported photos**, set various **import options, changed views** in the library, and made basic adjustments. Lastly, you adjusted the Lightroom interface, and used **keyboard shortcuts** to improve efficiency.

### Unit 2

In this unit, you learned how to **flag, rate, stack,** and **cull photos by using Survey view**. You **created and manipulated keywords**. You also created specific collections of photos by using **the Collections panel**, and quickly assembled a temporary **Quick Collection**. You filtered the photos visible in Grid view by entering criteria in **the Find panel**. You **synchronized develop settings** within a group of selected photos and **synchronized metadata adjustments**. Lastly, you learned to export photos in various formats.

### Unit 3

In this unit, you applied a preset from **the Presets panel** to a photo. You **adjusted white balance** and made basic tonal adjustments by using **the Histogram and Basic panels**. You also used steps in **the History panel** to revert a photo to a previous version, and **created snapshots** of a photo. You compared before and after versions of a photo. You used **a tone curve** to make precise tonal adjustments and made shadow and highlight adjustments by using **the Histogram and Tone Curve panels**. You used **the HSL/Color/Grayscale panel group** to adjust color in a photo. You converted photos to grayscale and adjusted them by using **the Grayscale panel**. You also created a split tone effect by using **the Split Toning panel**. You used options in the toolbar to crop and straighten photos, and made precise sharpening and noise reduction adjustments by using the options in **the Detail panel**. Lastly, you duplicated adjustments to other photos by copying and pasting them, synchronizing them, and creating custom presets.

### Unit 4

In this unit, you previewed a basic slideshow by using several techniques. You made **stroke and cast shadow adjustments** and created a **color-wash background**. You saved custom slide settings as a template in **the Template Browser panel**. You also added **text and rating overlays** to slides and used **guides** to position and crop photos against a background. Lastly, you made **basic playback adjustments**, such as slide and transition duration, and you **exported** a final slideshow as a PDF.

**Unit 5**

In this topic, you adjusted the way photos are prepared for printing. You **created both single and multiple photo layouts**, including **rotating** and **cropping** photos, setting up **borderless prints**, and saving custom layouts as **templates**. You also set specific output options, including **basic printing settings** and **managing color** both within Lightroom and using a specific printer.

**Unit 6**

In this unit, you created **a Flash-based web gallery**. You selected the photos to include in the gallery, added **descriptive gallery text**, adjusted **the gallery layout** and colors, and added **metadata photo information**. You also **previewed** a gallery in a Web browser to ensure it looked the way you intended, and you learned how to **upload** a gallery to a host server by using FTP options within Lightroom.

# Topic B: Continued learning after class

It is impossible to learn to use any software effectively in a single day. To get the most out of this class, you should begin working with Adobe Photoshop Lightroom to perform real tasks as soon as possible. We also offer resources for continued learning.

## Next courses in this series

This is the only course in this series.

## Other resources

For more information, visit www.axzopress.com.

# Lightroom 1.0

## Quick reference

| Button | Shortcut keys | Function |
| --- | --- | --- |
| | CTRL + ALT + 1, 2, 3, 4, or 5 | Switches between modules: Library (1), Develop (2), Slideshow (3), Print (4), and Web (5) |
| | CTRL + ALT + ↑ | Returns to previous module |
| | G | Switches to Grid view |
| | E | Switches to Loupe view |
| | C | Switches to Compare view |
| | N | Switches to Survey view |
| | ← → | Selects the photo to the left or right of the currently selected photo |
| | SHIFT + ← or → | Selects the photo to the left or right in addition to the currently selected photo |
| | C + = | Zooms to the next higher magnification |
| | CTRL + – | Zooms to the next lower magnification |
| | Z | Toggles between 1:1 magnification and the previous magnification |
| | CTRL + D | Deselects all photos in the library |
| | SHIFT + CTRL + D | Deselects all photos except the active photo |
| | CTRL + Z | Undoes last change |
| | B | Adds photo to Quick Collection |
| | CTRL + B | Shows the Quick Collection |

| Button | Shortcut keys | Function |
|---|---|---|
| | ⓪, ①, ②, ③, ④, or ⑤ | Sets rating |
| | ⟨TAB⟩ | Collapses/expands both the left and right panel groups |
| | ⟨CTRL⟩ + ⟨TAB⟩ | Collapses/expands all four interface elements surrounding the center pane |
| | ⟨L⟩ repeatedly | Toggles between Lights Dim mode, Lights Out mode, and Lights On mode |
| | ⟨F⟩ repeatedly | Toggles between Standard screen mode and Fullscreen with Menu mode |

# Glossary

**Backdrop**

The screen area outside the boundaries of a photo.

**Borderless photos**

Photos that bleed off the edge of the paper. Borderless printing saves you from having to trim photos after they've been printed.

**Chromatic aberration**

Color fringes that appear in photos, particularly at high-contrast edges. The fringes are typically caused by camera lens distortions.

**Clipping**

The result of increasing or decreasing the contrast too much in a photo. The bad contrast converts multiple brightness levels to a single shade, which causes the loss of detail.

**Collection**

A feature in Lightroom that you can use to group photos that are in different folders.

**Color cast**

A color that appears subtly throughout an image and that might be particularly noticeable in areas that should be neutral.

**Color wash**

A gradient of two colors; the color you select for the color wash and the color of the background.

**Highlight tones**

The lightest pixel tones in a photo.

**IPTC (International Press Telecommunications Council)**

A catalog system designed to combine text and photos together as a way to help photographers organize and market their work.

**Keywords**

A specific type of metadata. Keywords are words you can attach to photos in order to manage them more effectively.

**Keyword Set**

A large collection of keywords grouped together in a set.

**Metadata**

Information, such as keywords or descriptions, you can attach to photos.

**Noise**

Undesirable flecks of random color in a portion of a photo that should consist of smooth color.

**Rule of Thirds**

A principle of composition that involves creating a grid over a photo consisting of two evenly spaced horizontal vertical lines. The principle indicates you should position the photo subject where the lines intersect.

**Shadow tones**

The darkest pixel tones in a photo.

**Tonal Range**

The maximum range of tones visible in a photo. The difference between a photo's maximum highlight pixel and its minimum shadow pixel.

**Vignetting**

The darkening at the outsides of the photo frame. The darkening is typically caused by camera lens distortion.

**White balance**

The process of removing unrealistic color casts in a photo, so that objects that appear white in person are rendered white in your photo.

# Index